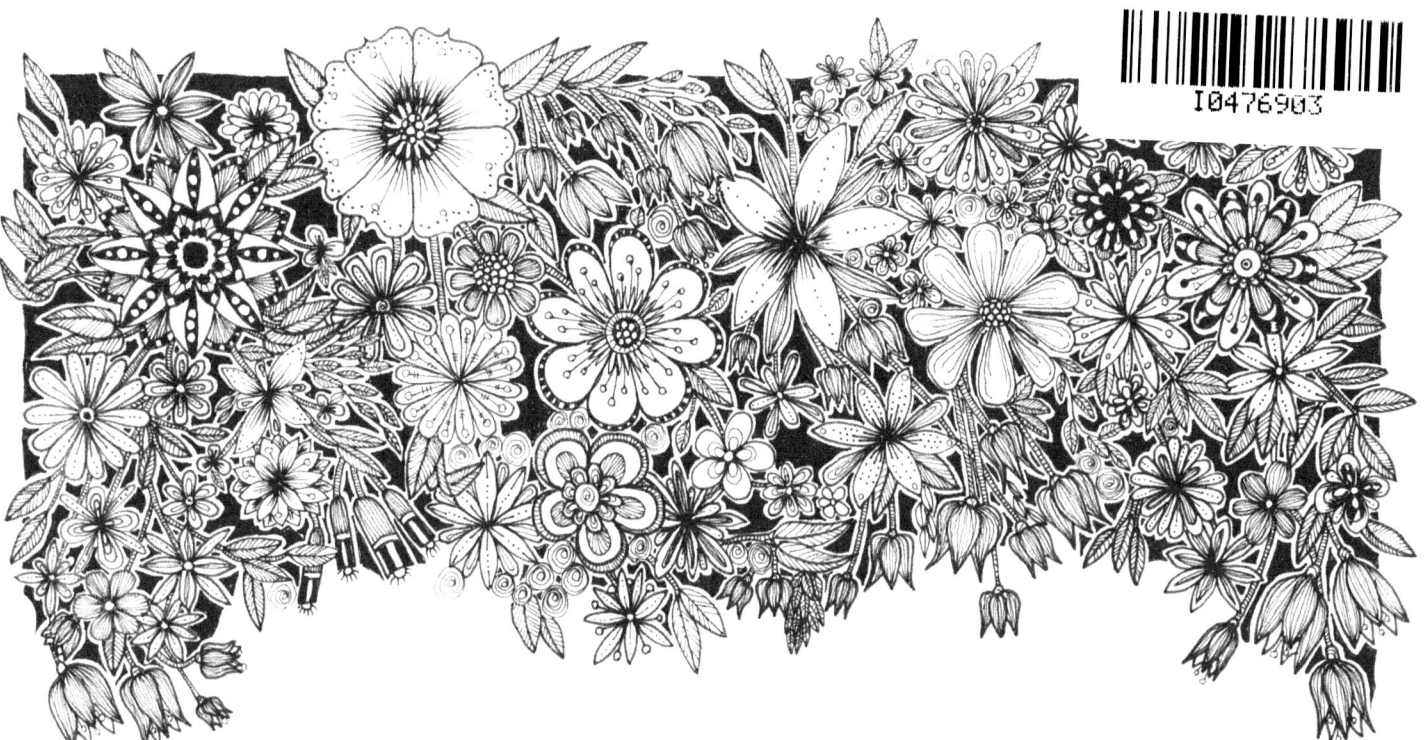

I0476903

Colors of Whimsy

I'd like to thank my husband and family for their support in making this coloring book.
I'd also like to thank Maria Wedel for the kick start
to get my work published and into the hands of people who love to color.
Bev Choy

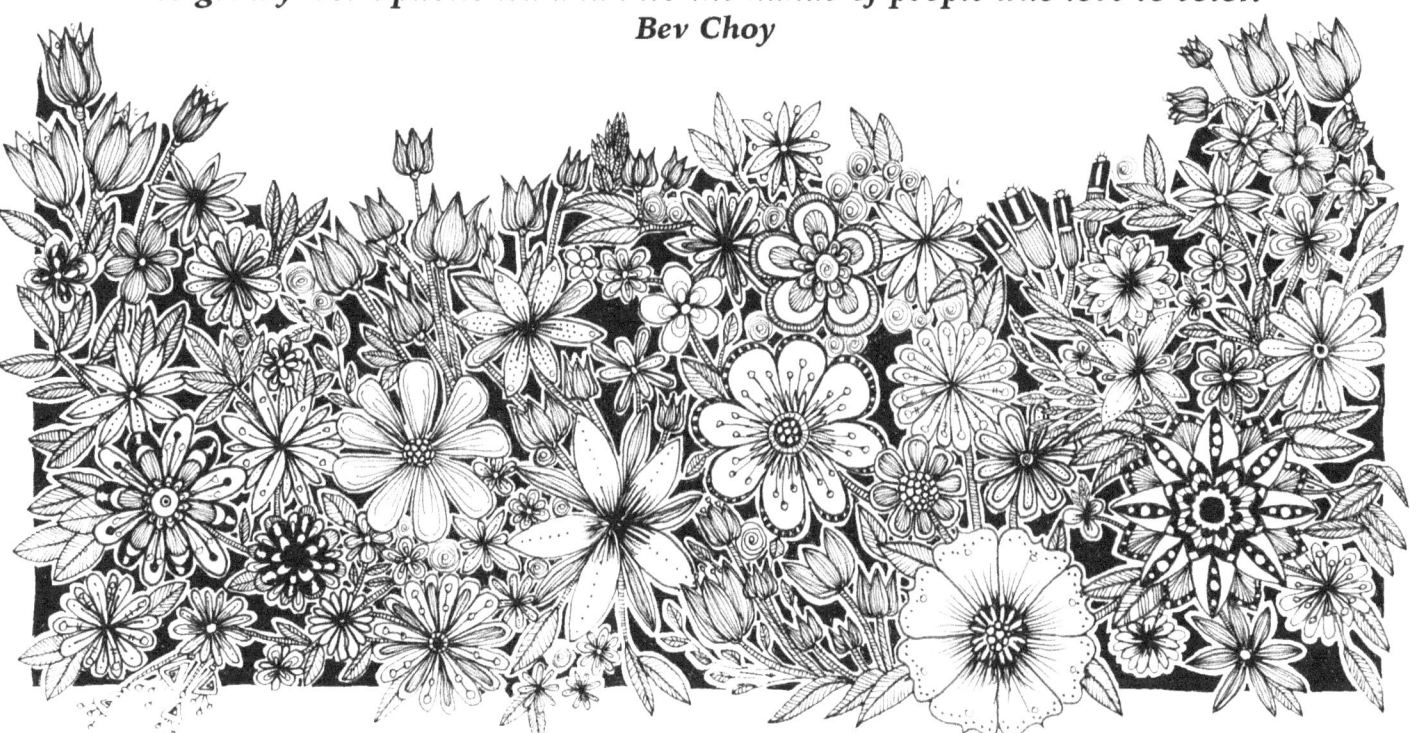

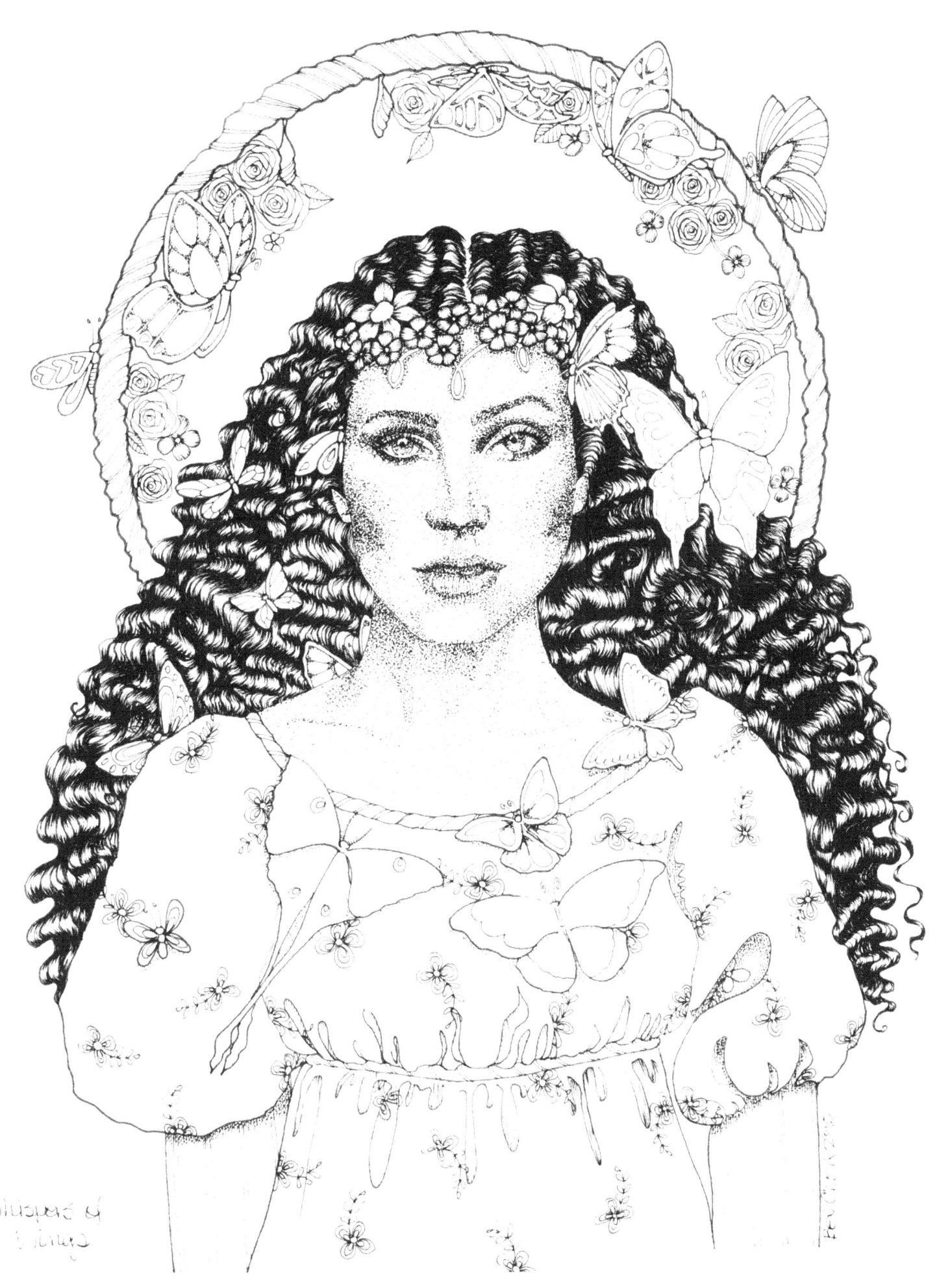

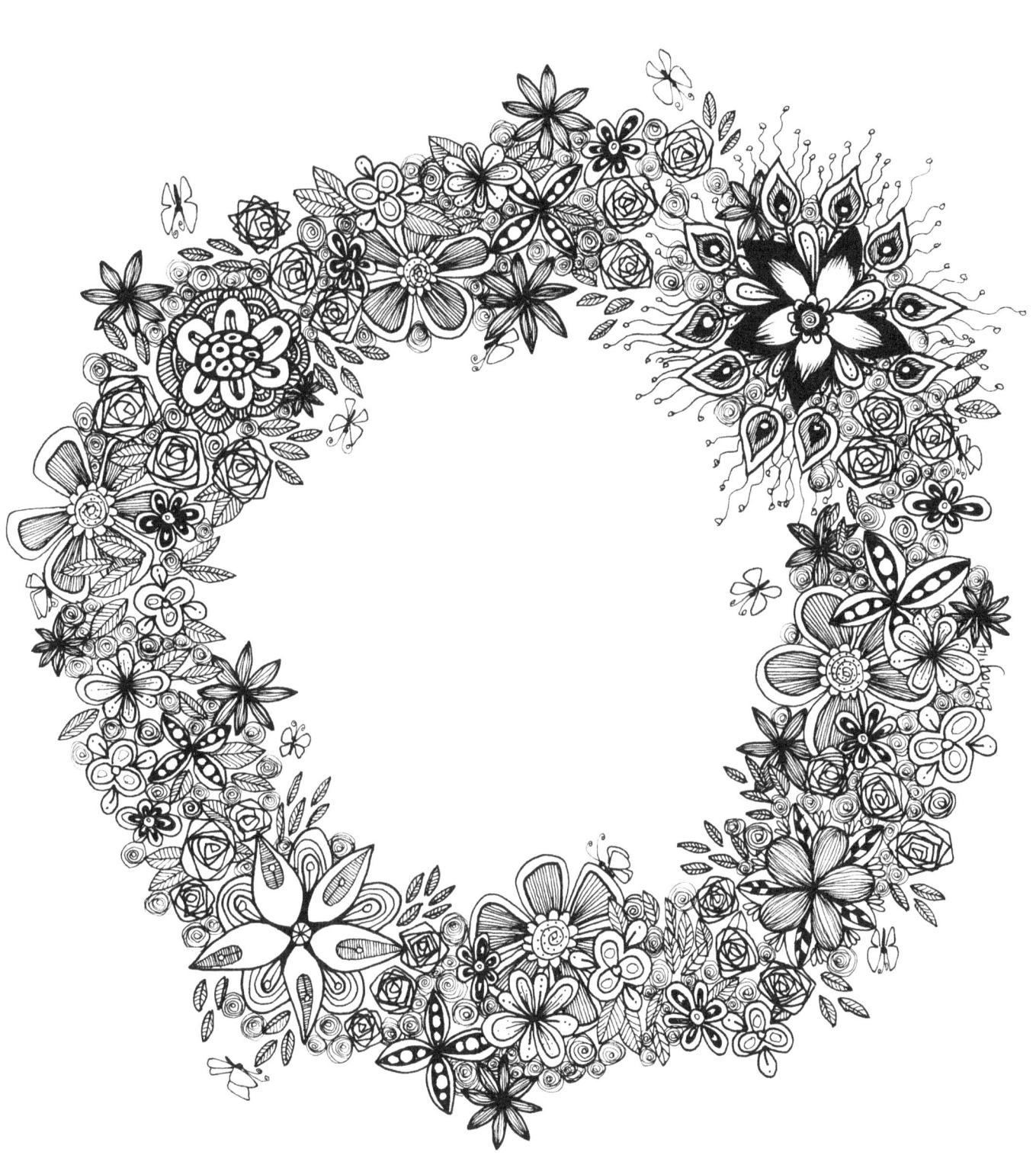

...— BUTTERFLY GARDEN —...

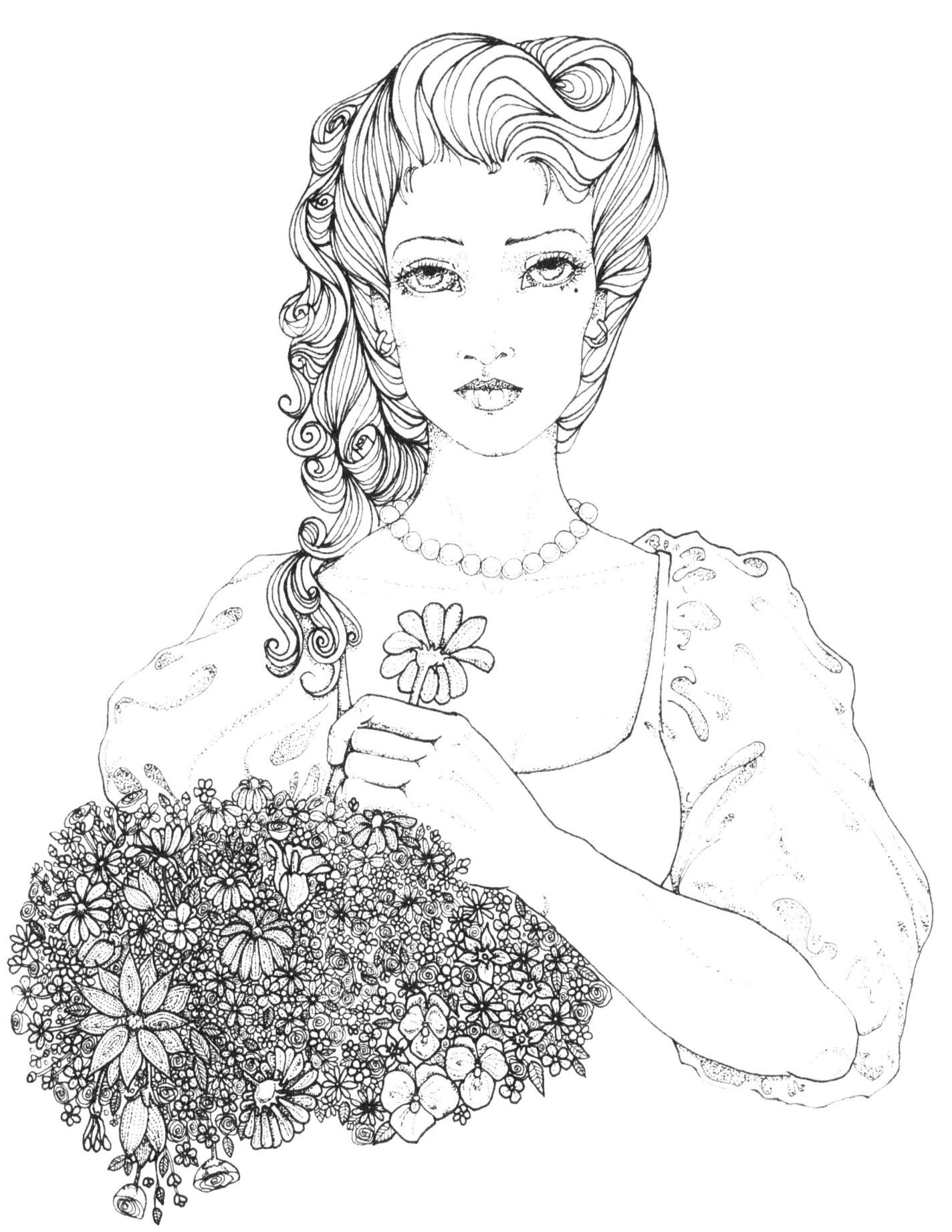

BEV CHOY 2015

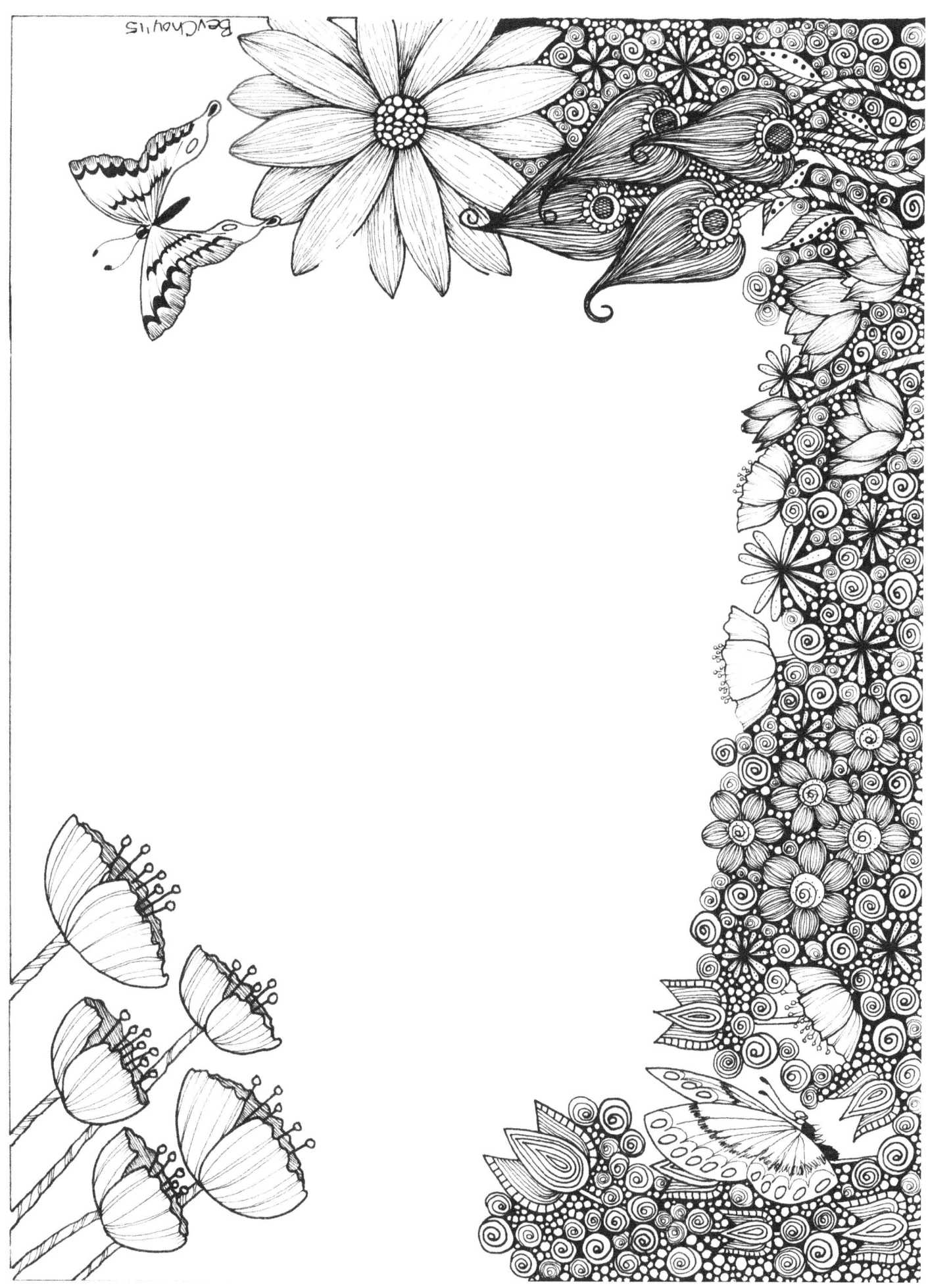

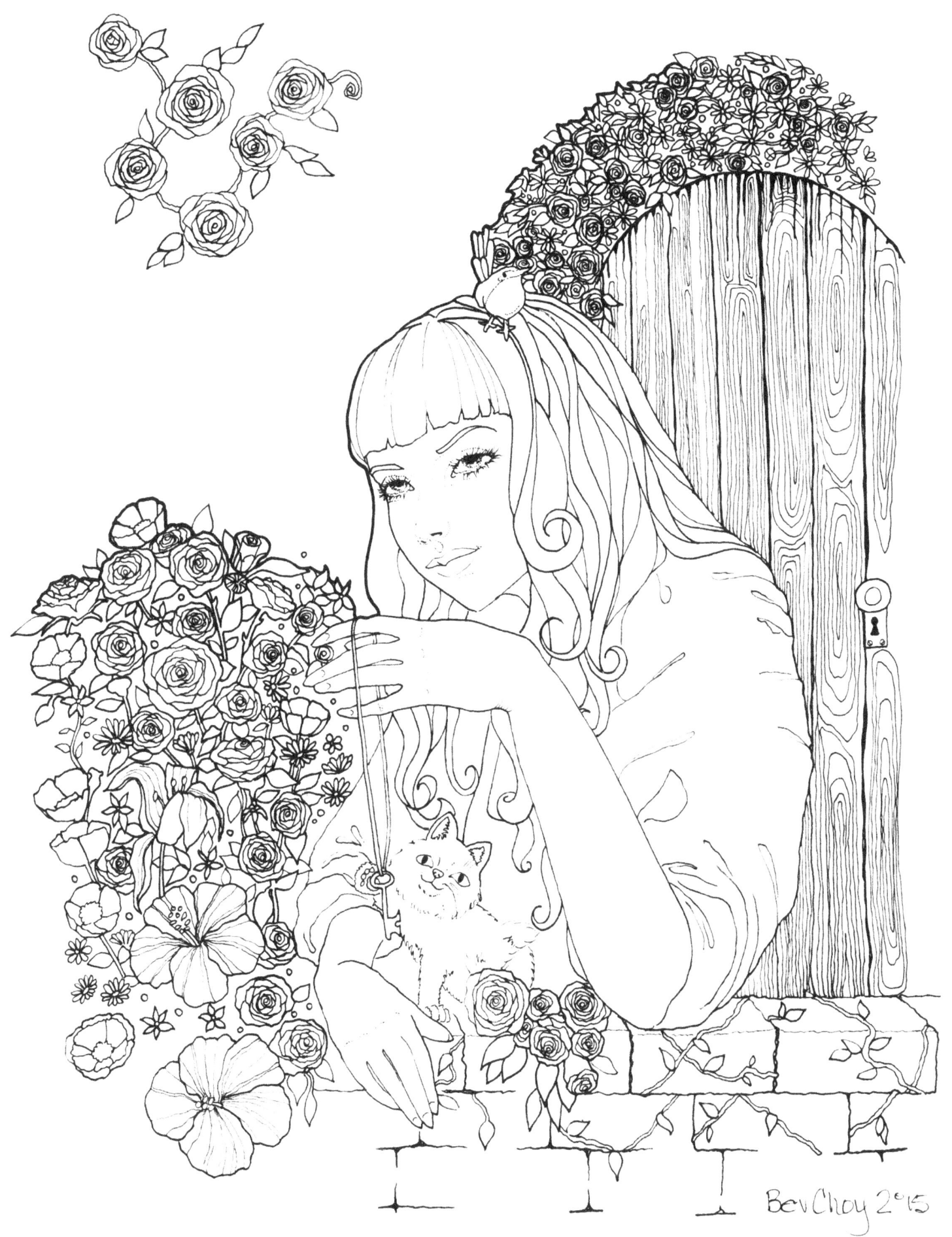

Bev Choy 2015

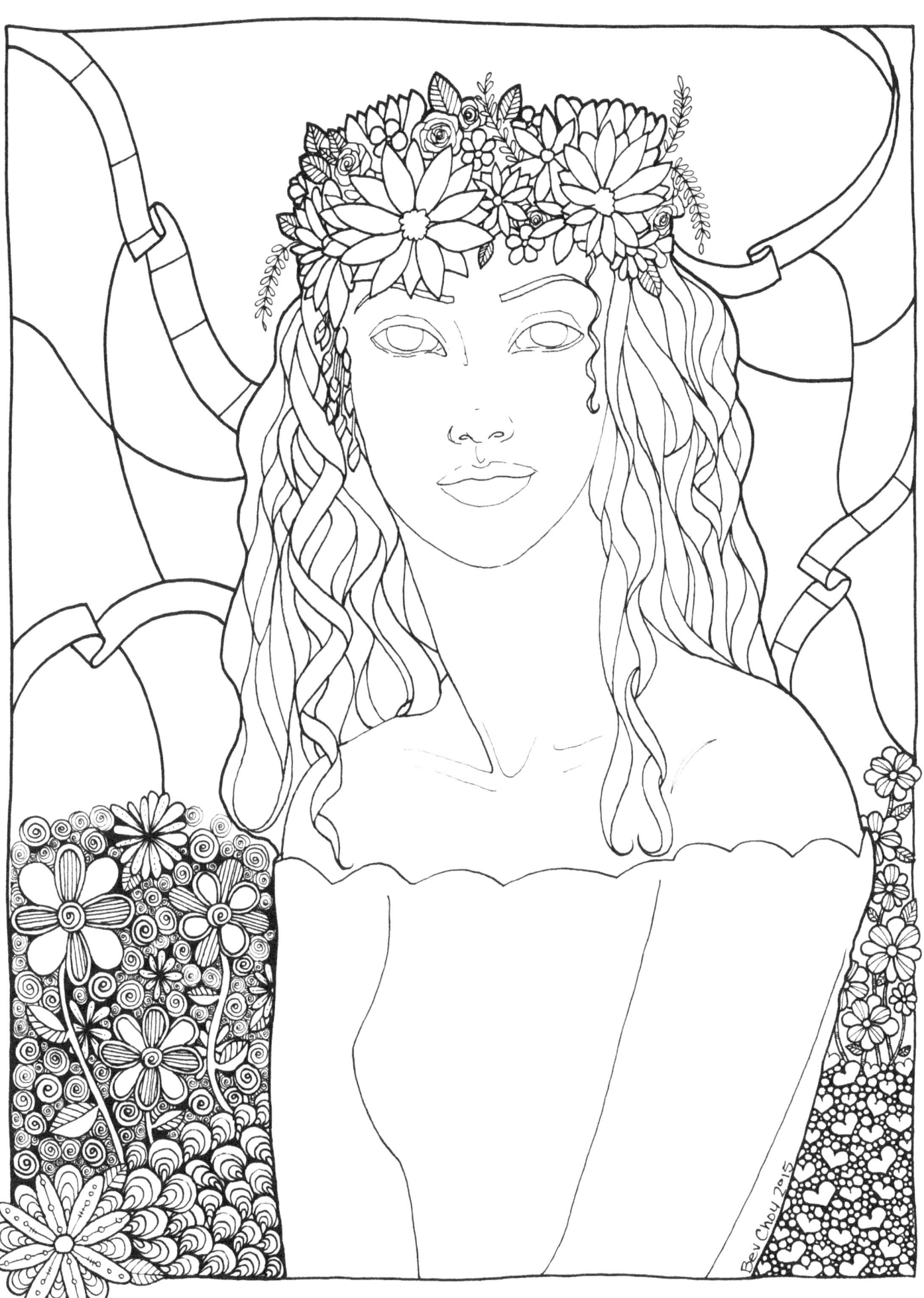

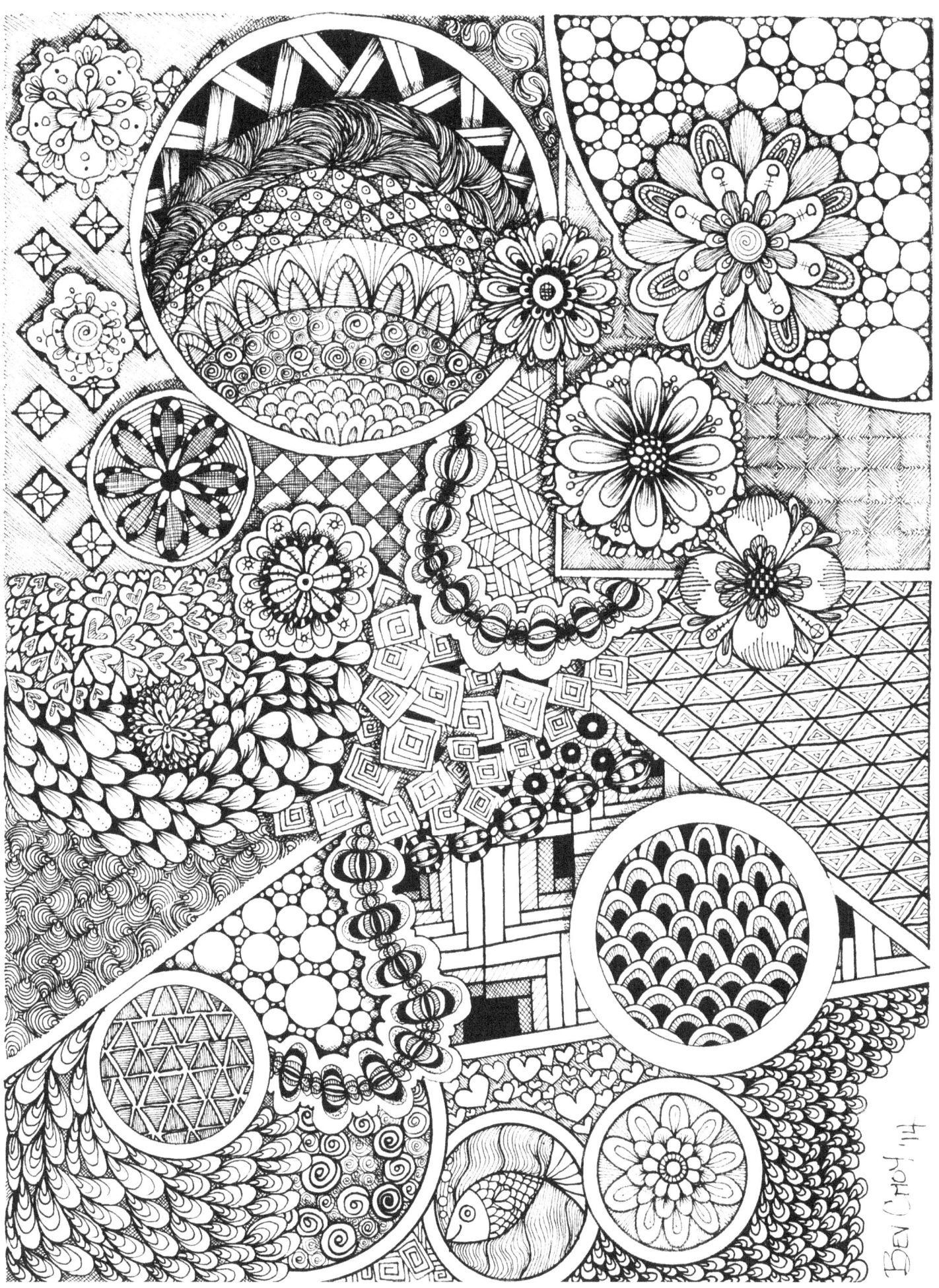

Bev Choy '14

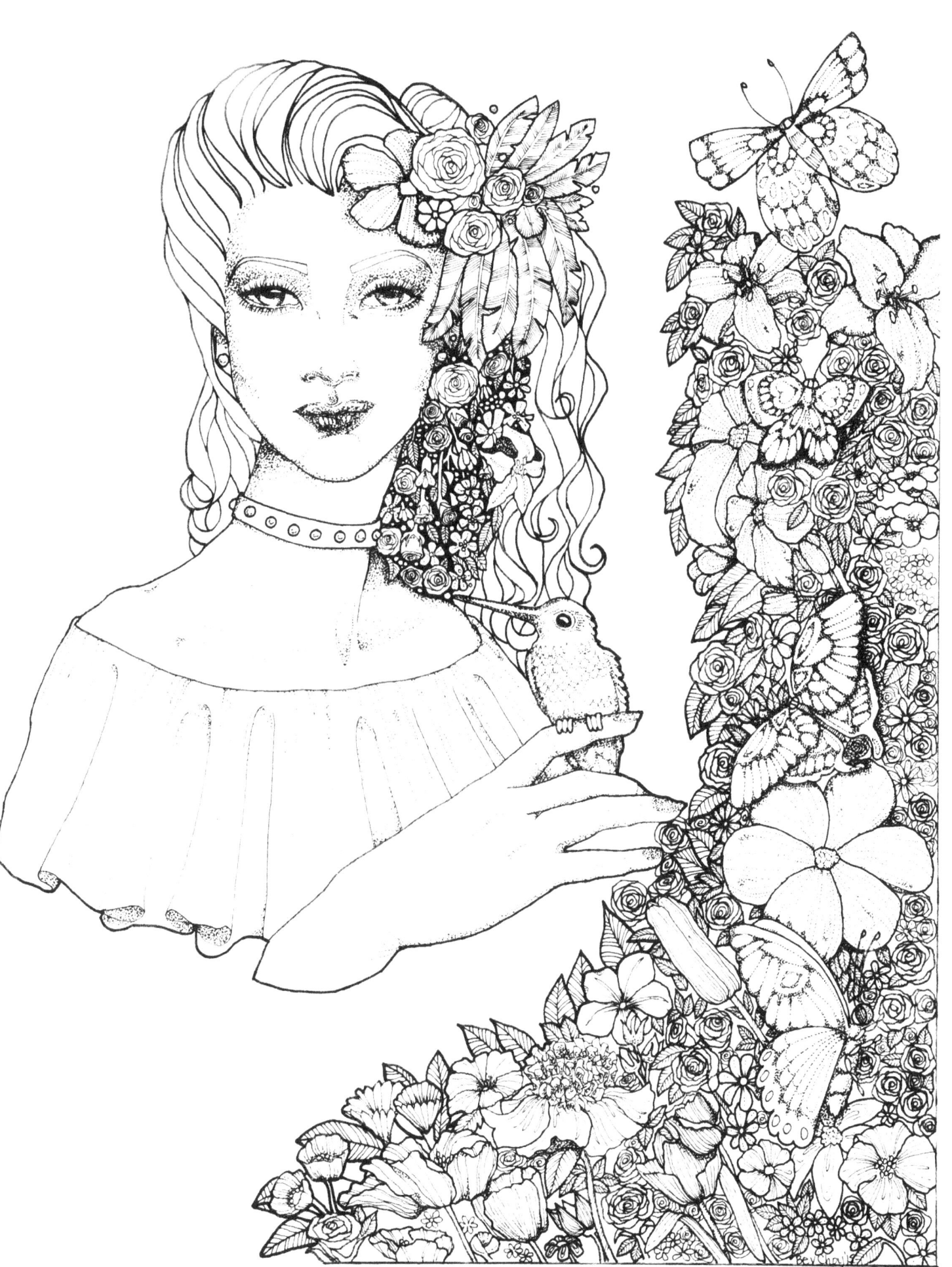

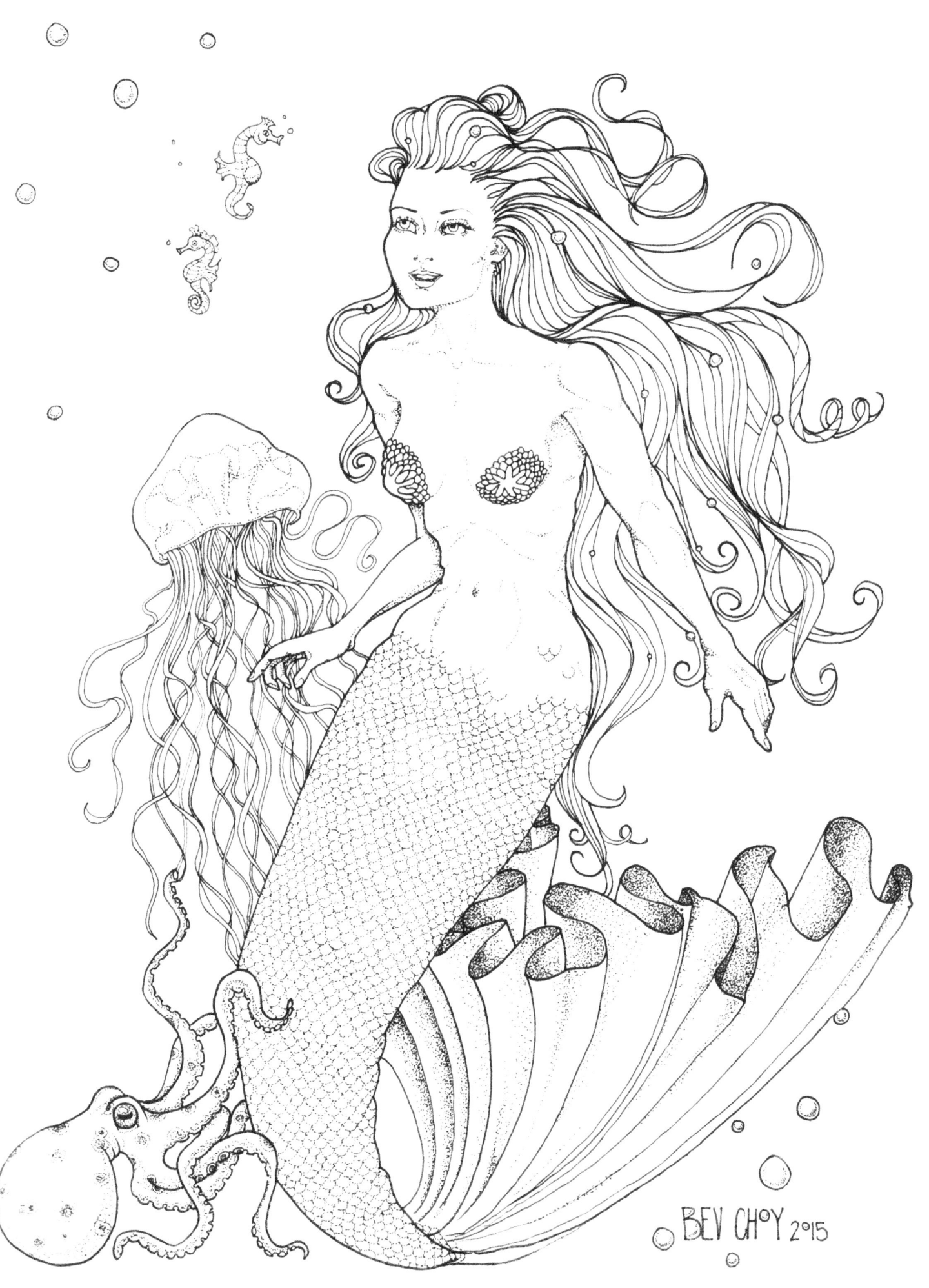

BEV CHOY 2015

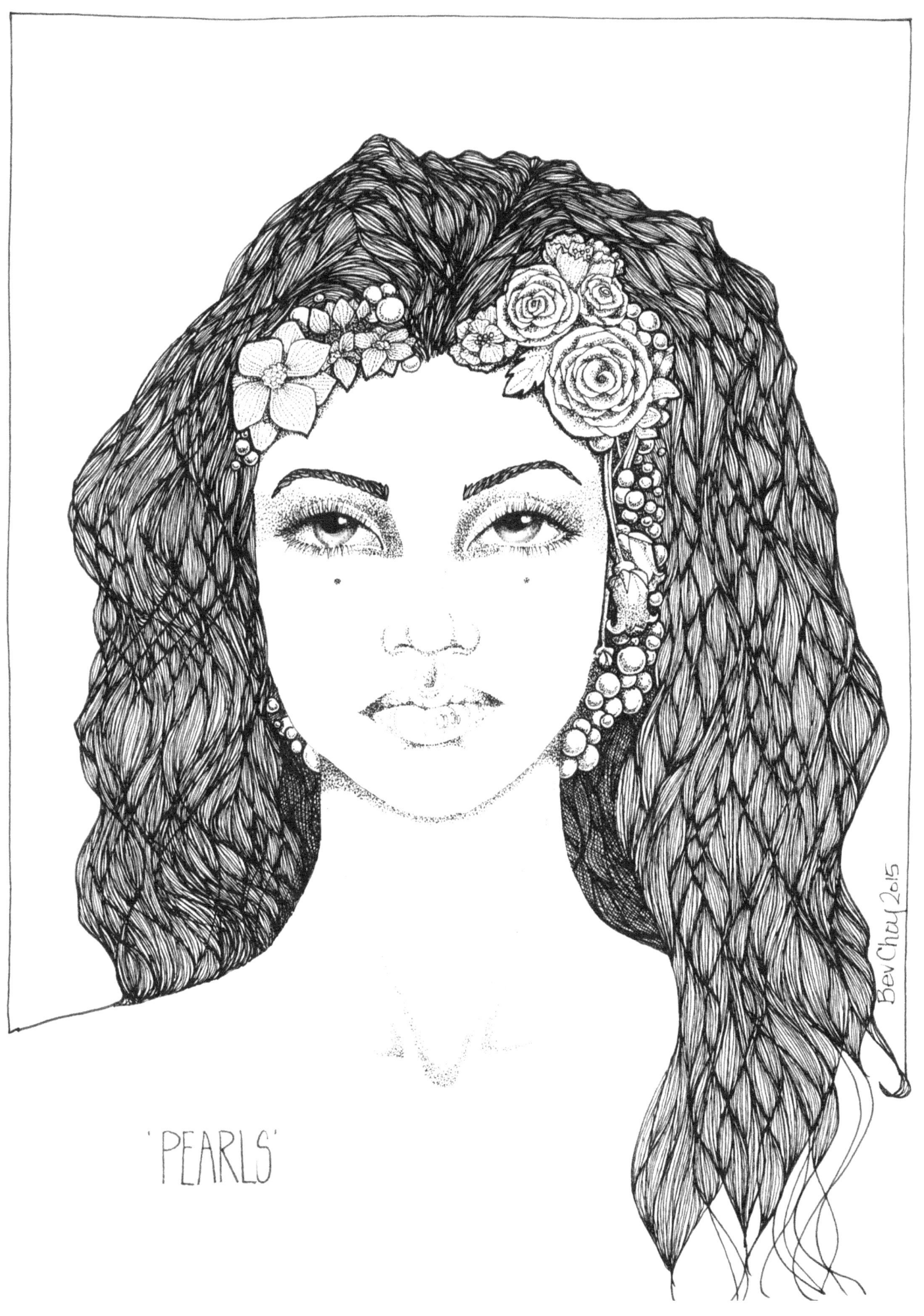

'PEARLS'

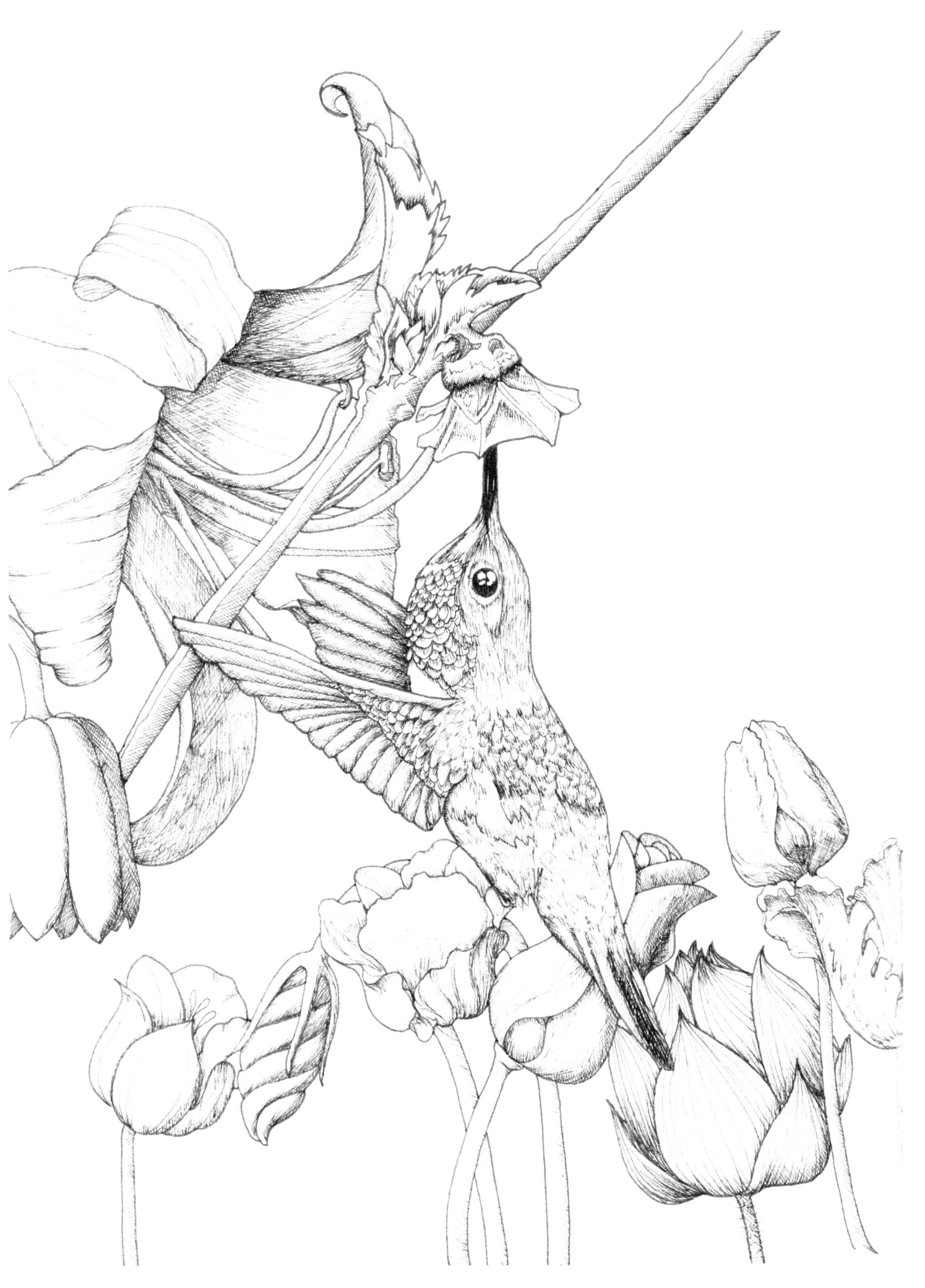

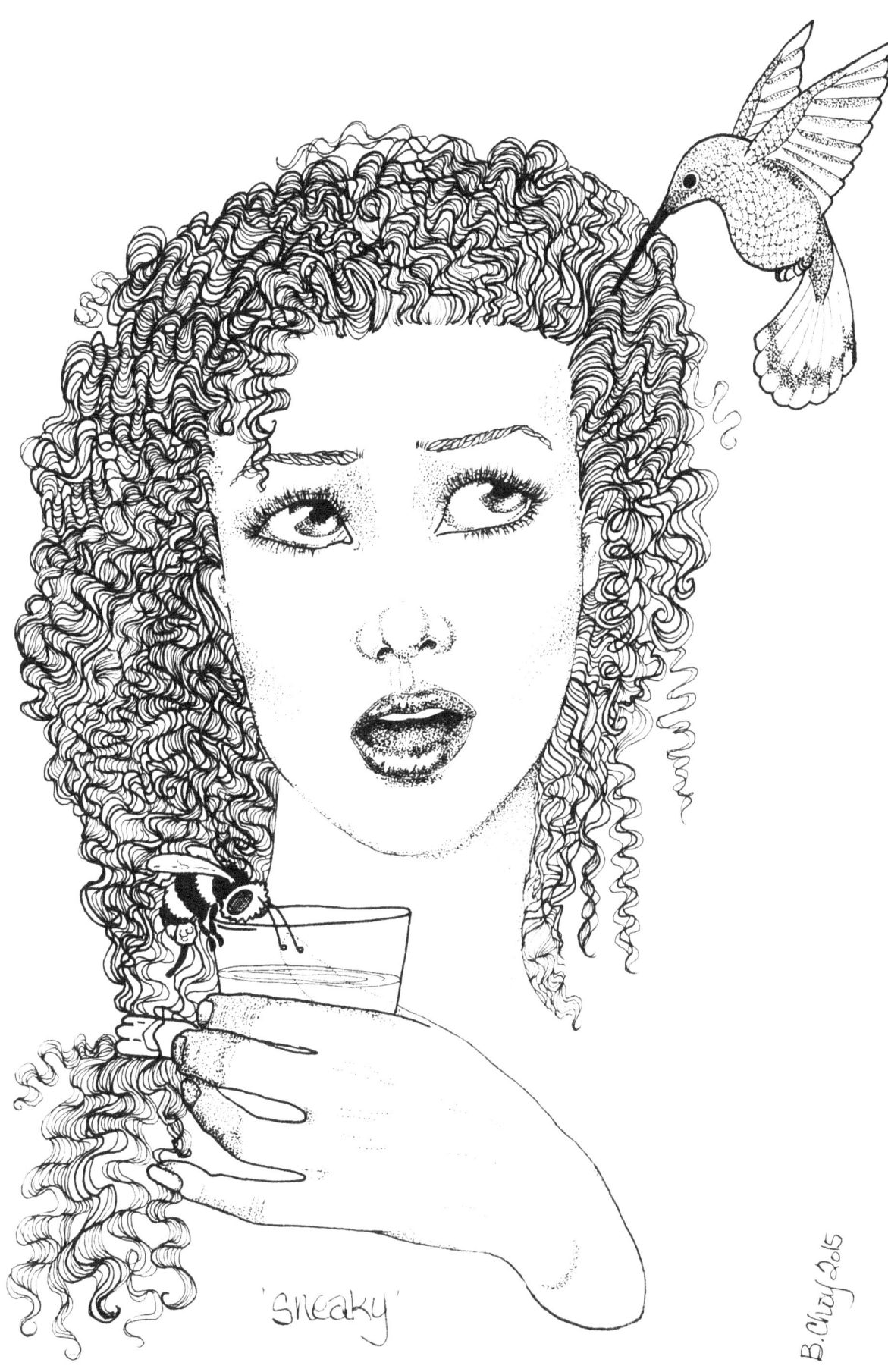

'Sneaky'

B.Clay 2015

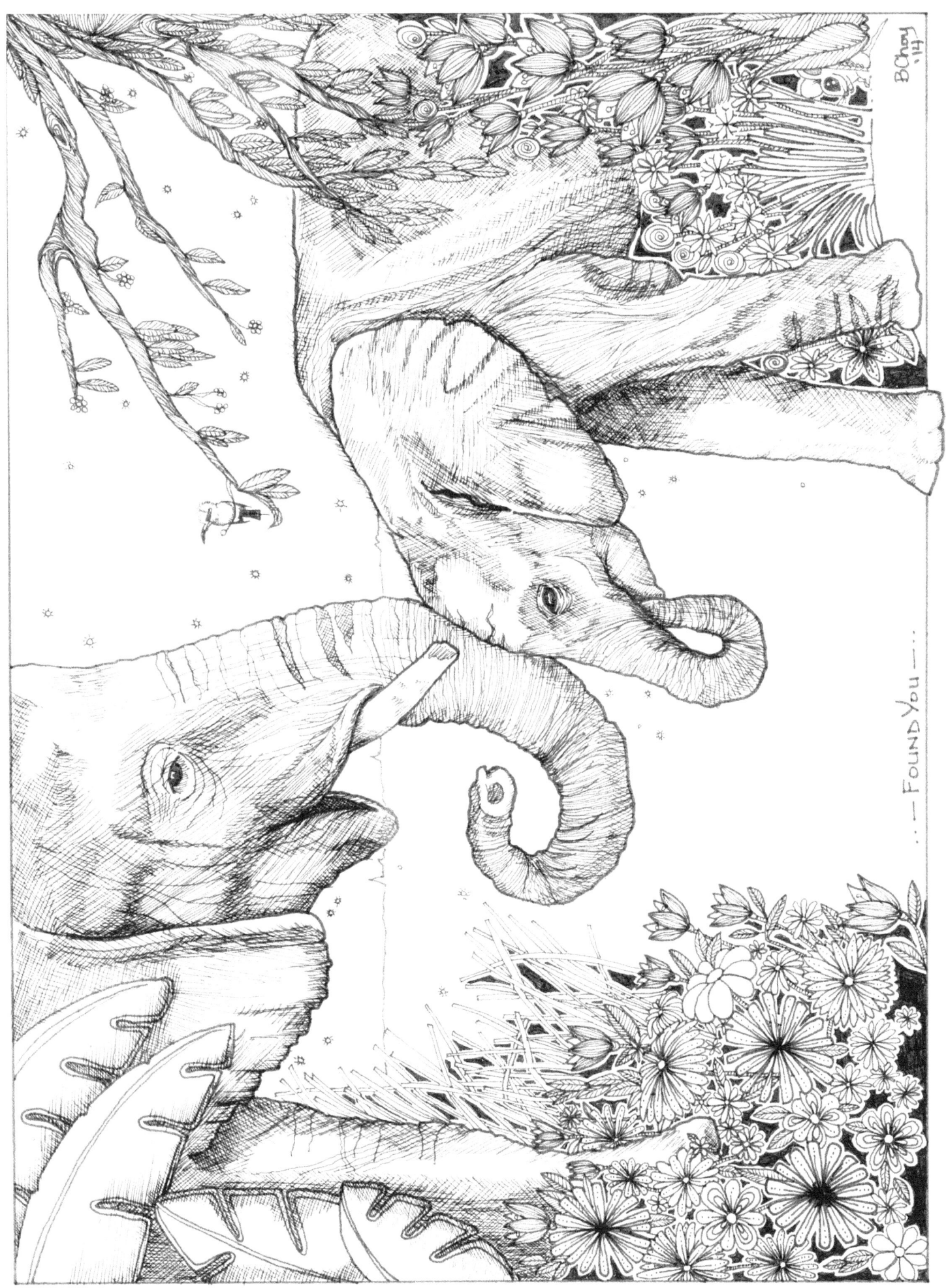

... — Found You —...

BChoy '14

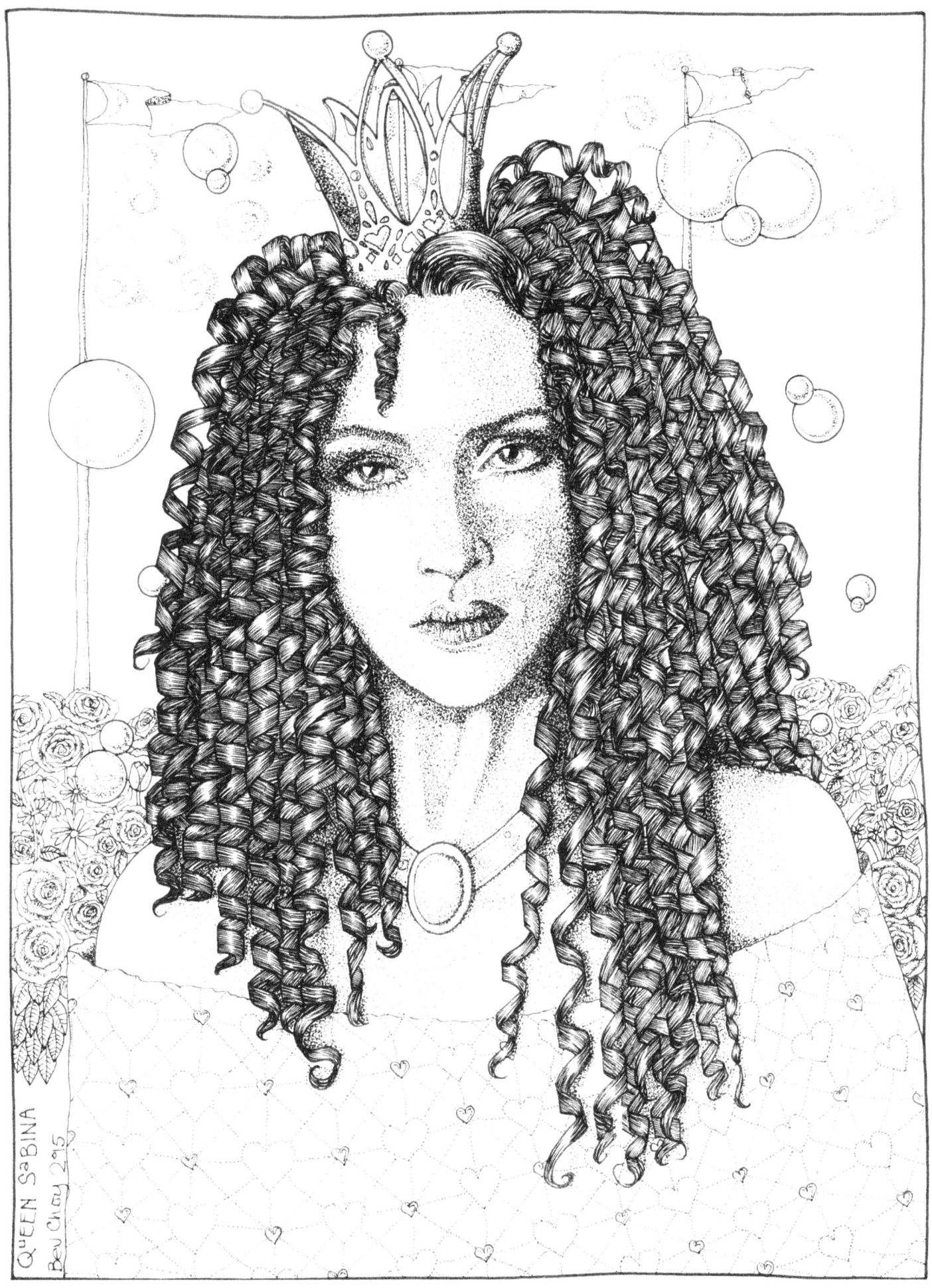

QUEEN SABINA
Ben Chay 2015

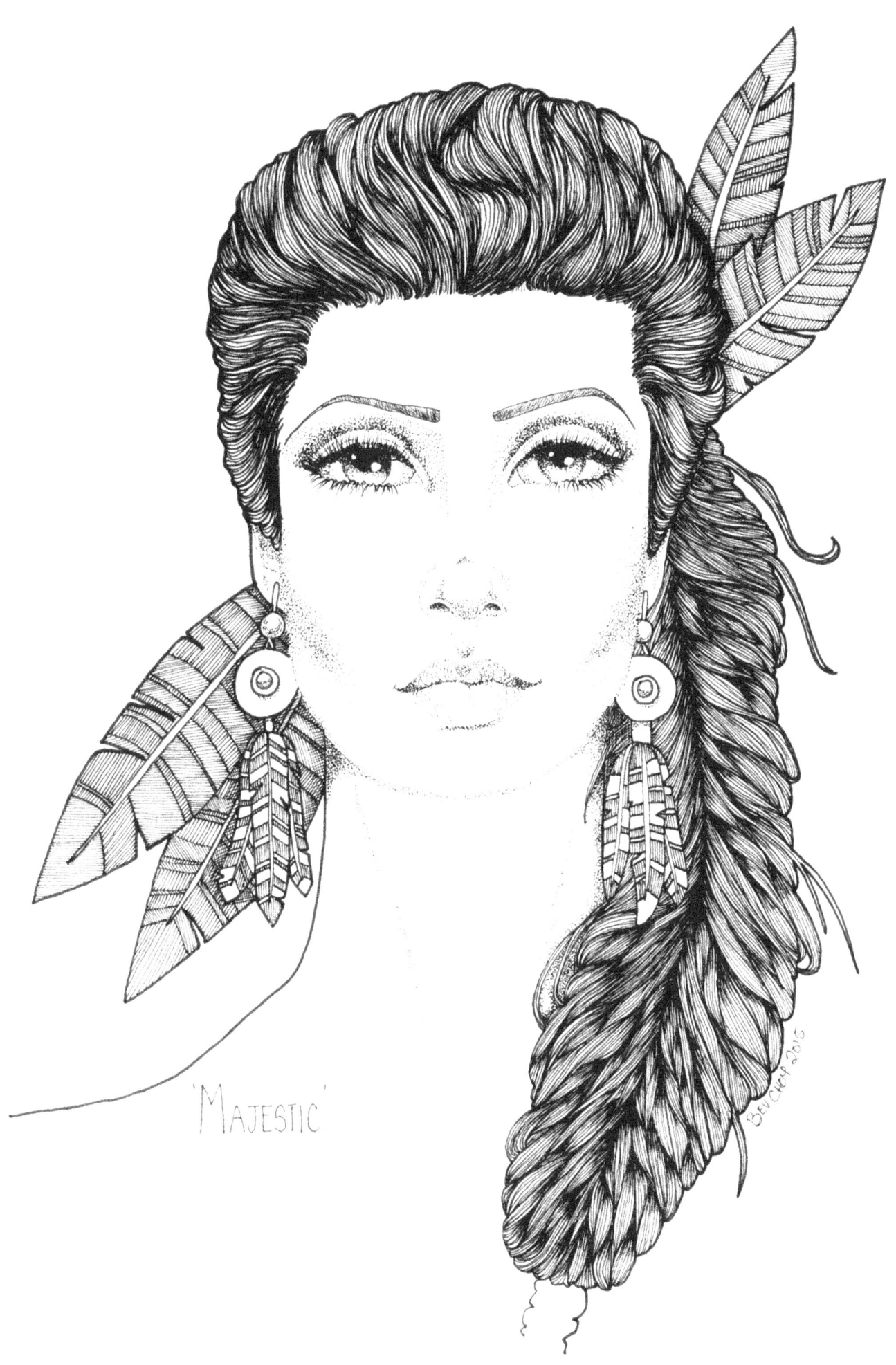

'Majestic'

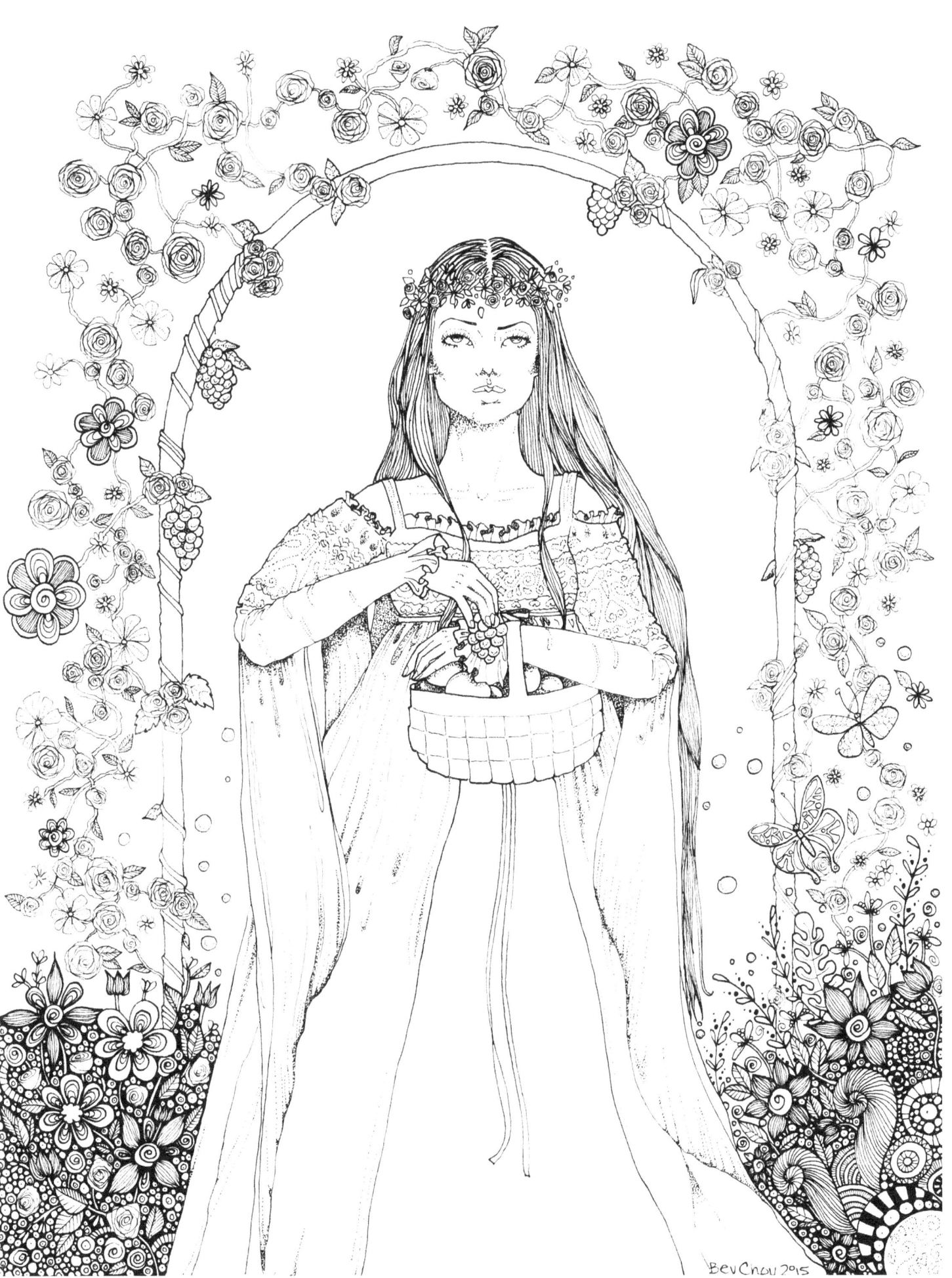

BevChou 2015

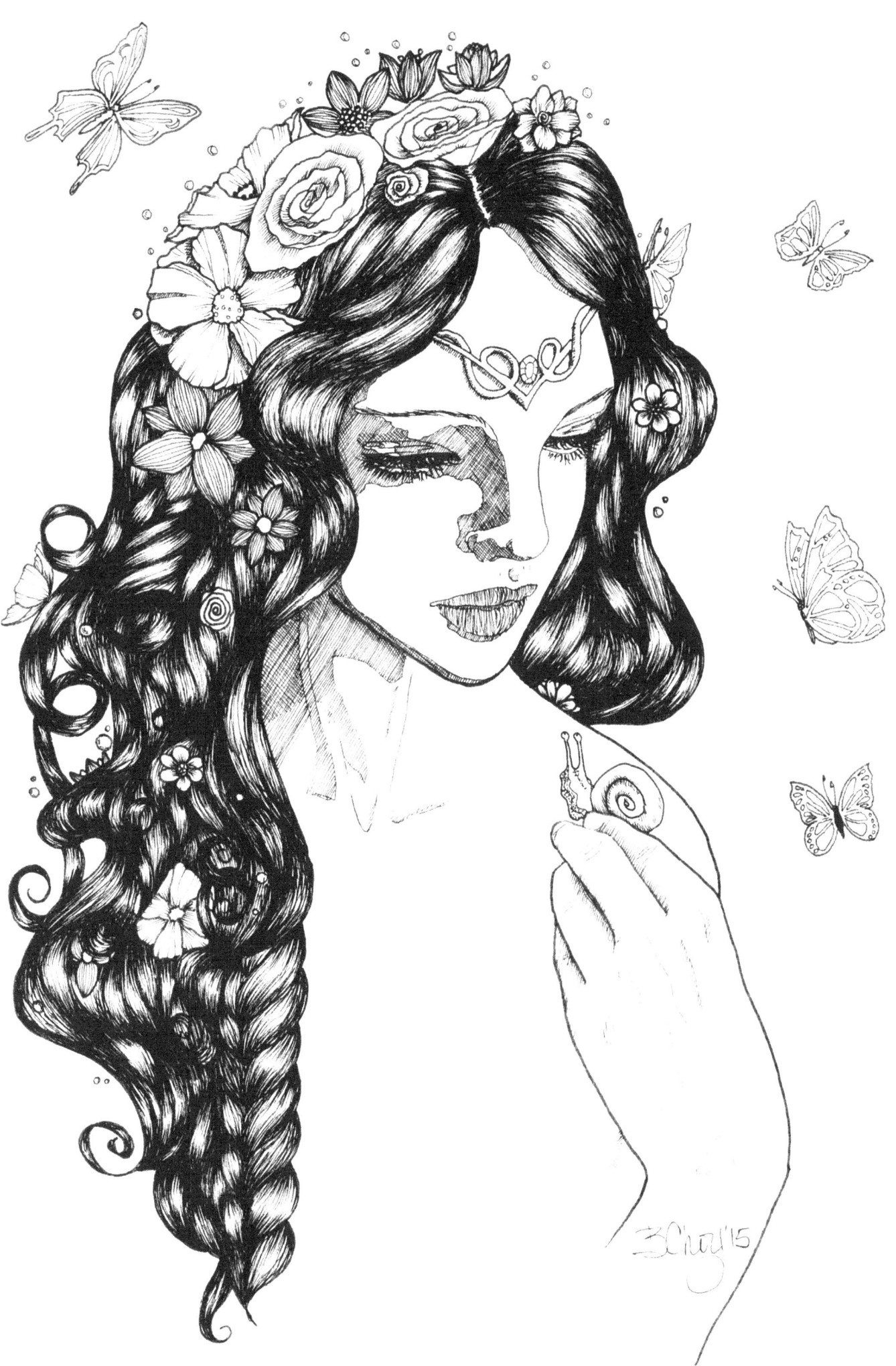

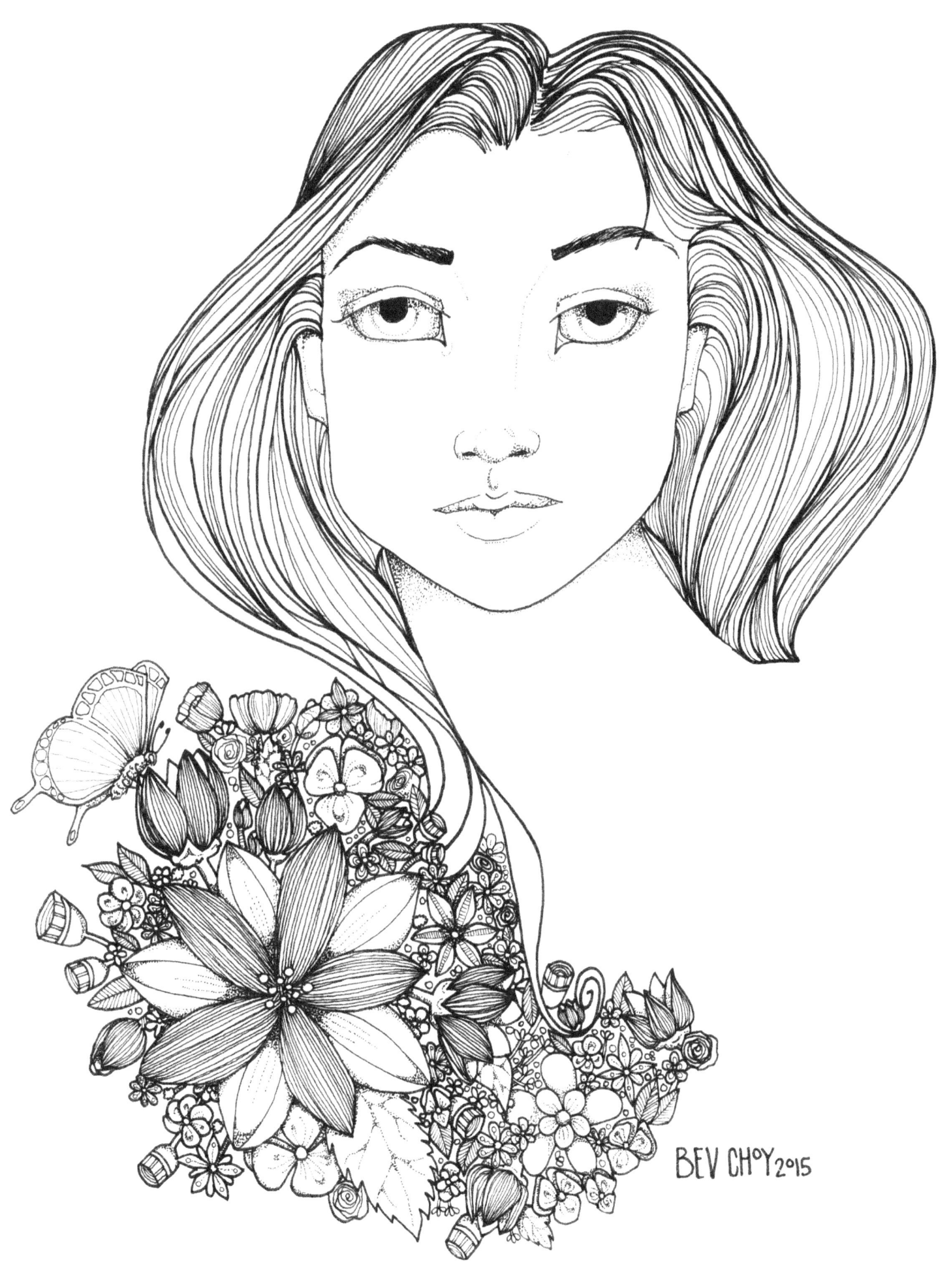

BEV CHOY 2015

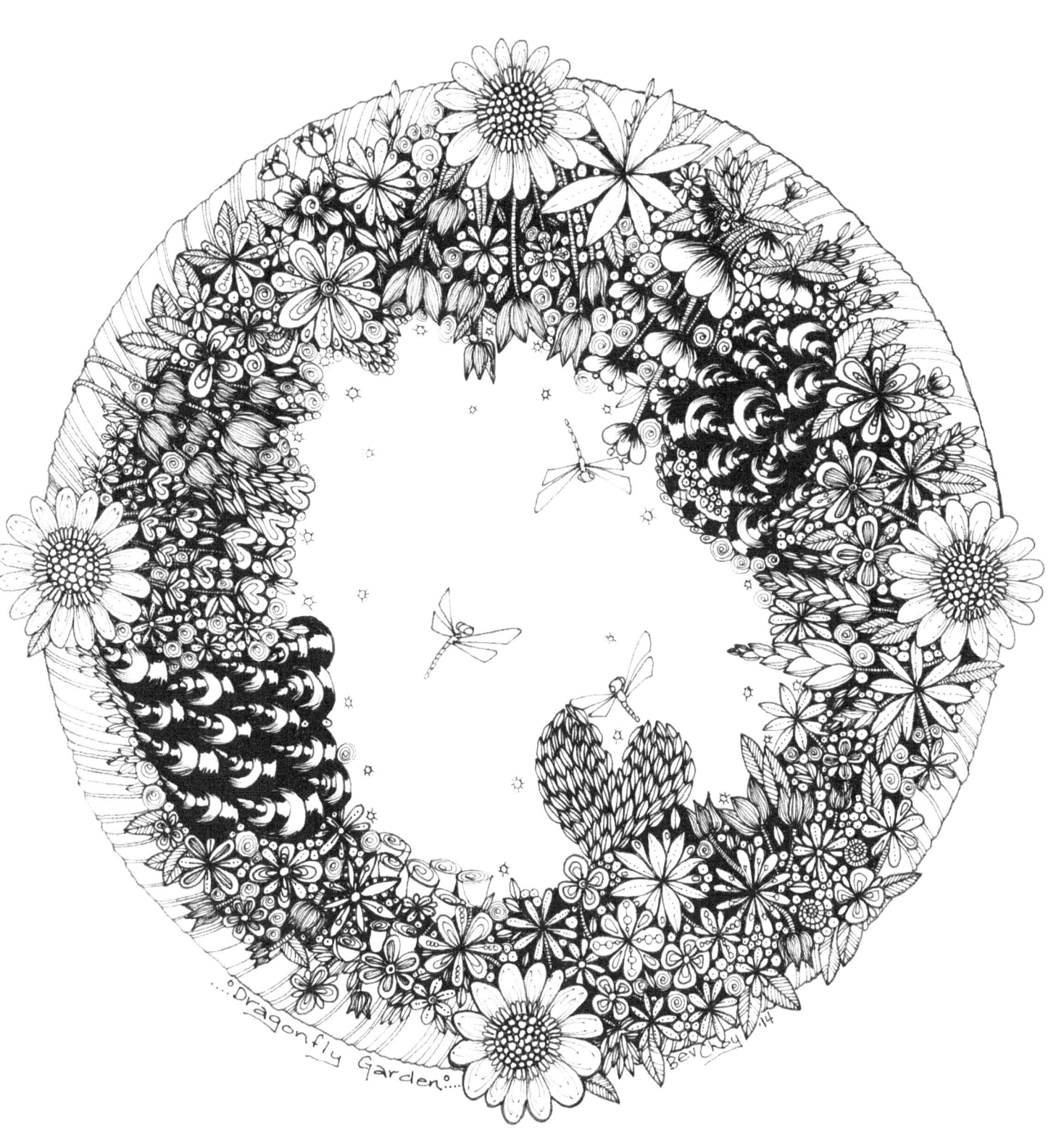

...°Dragonfly Garden°...

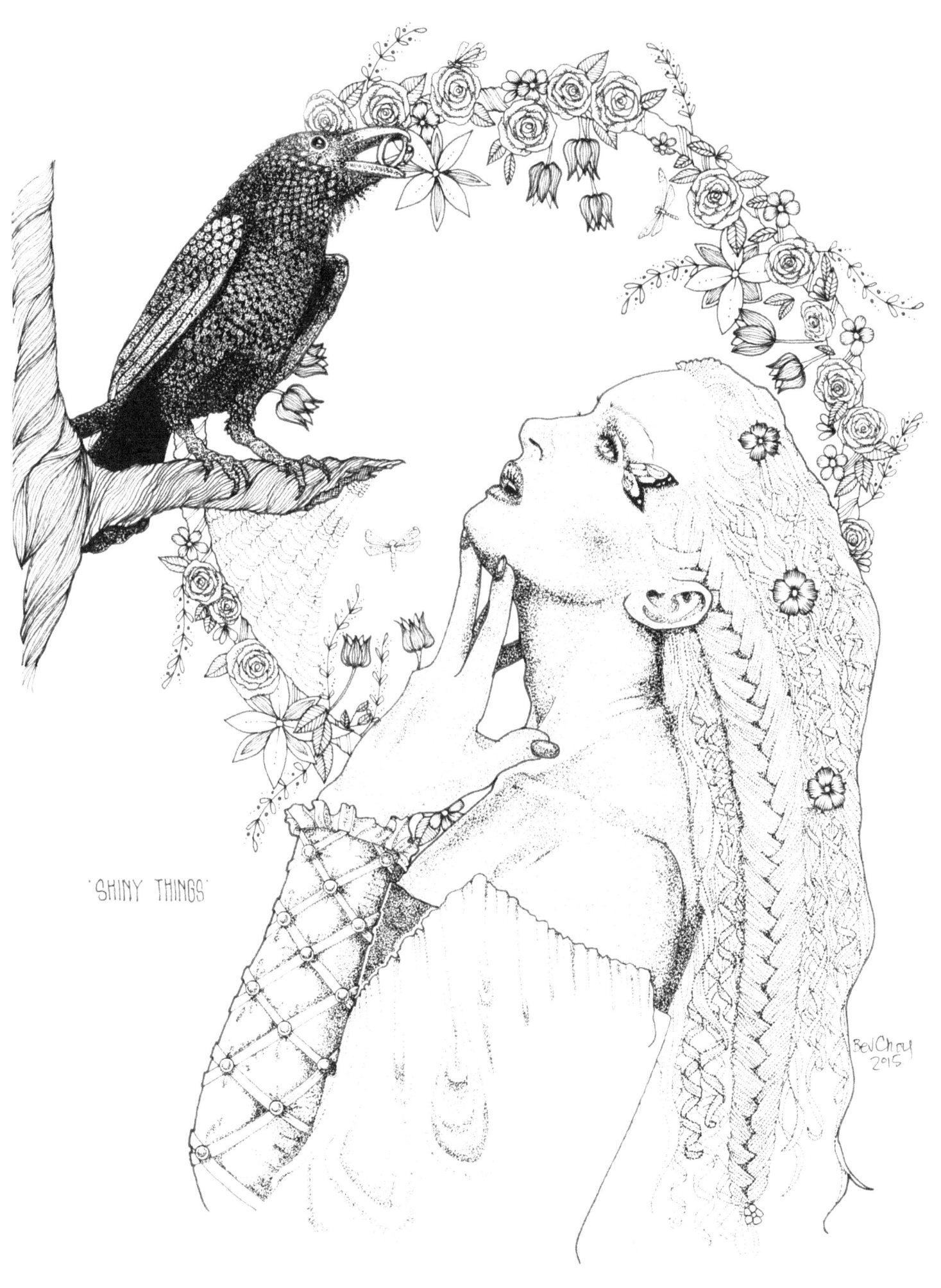

'SHINY THINGS'

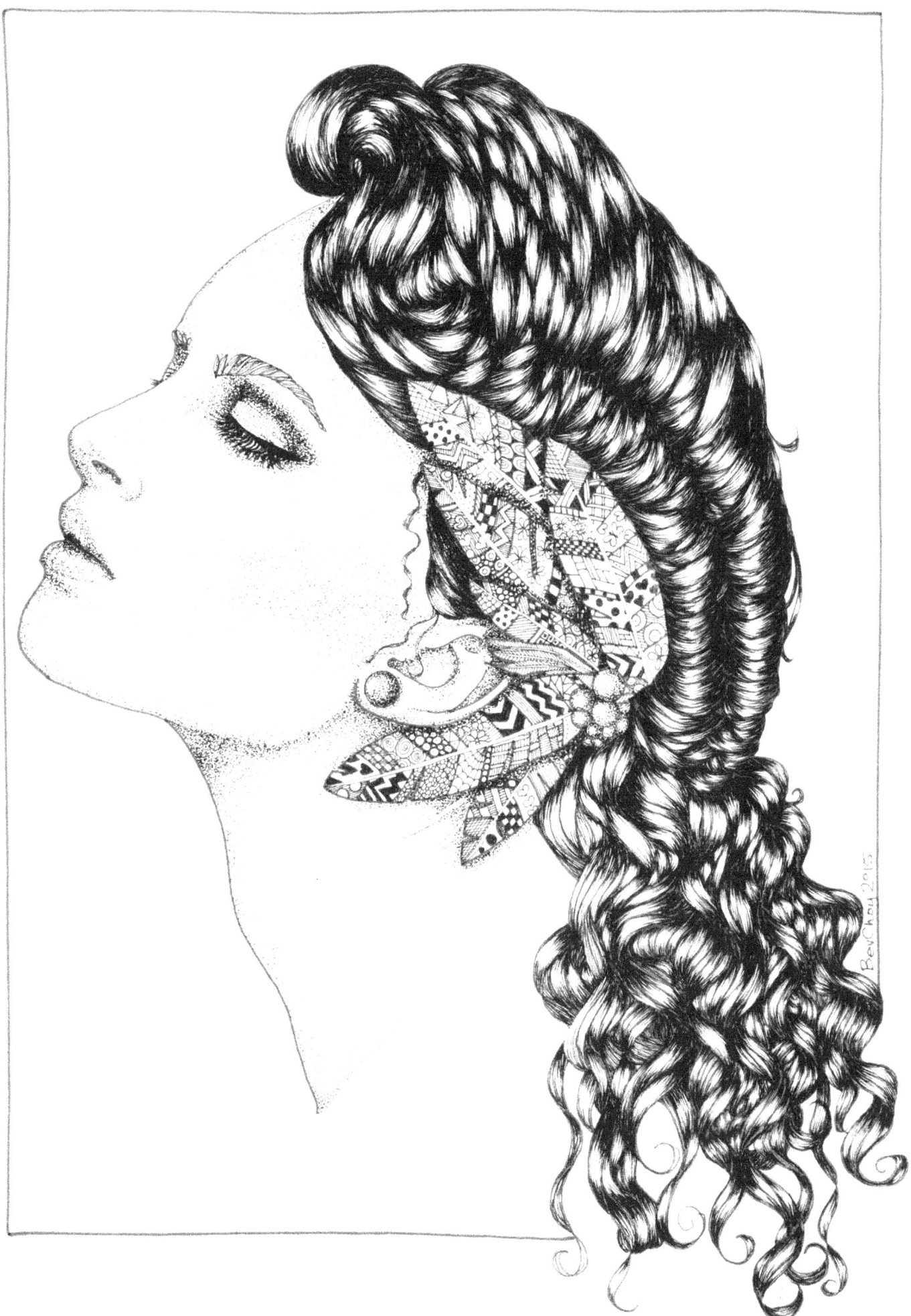

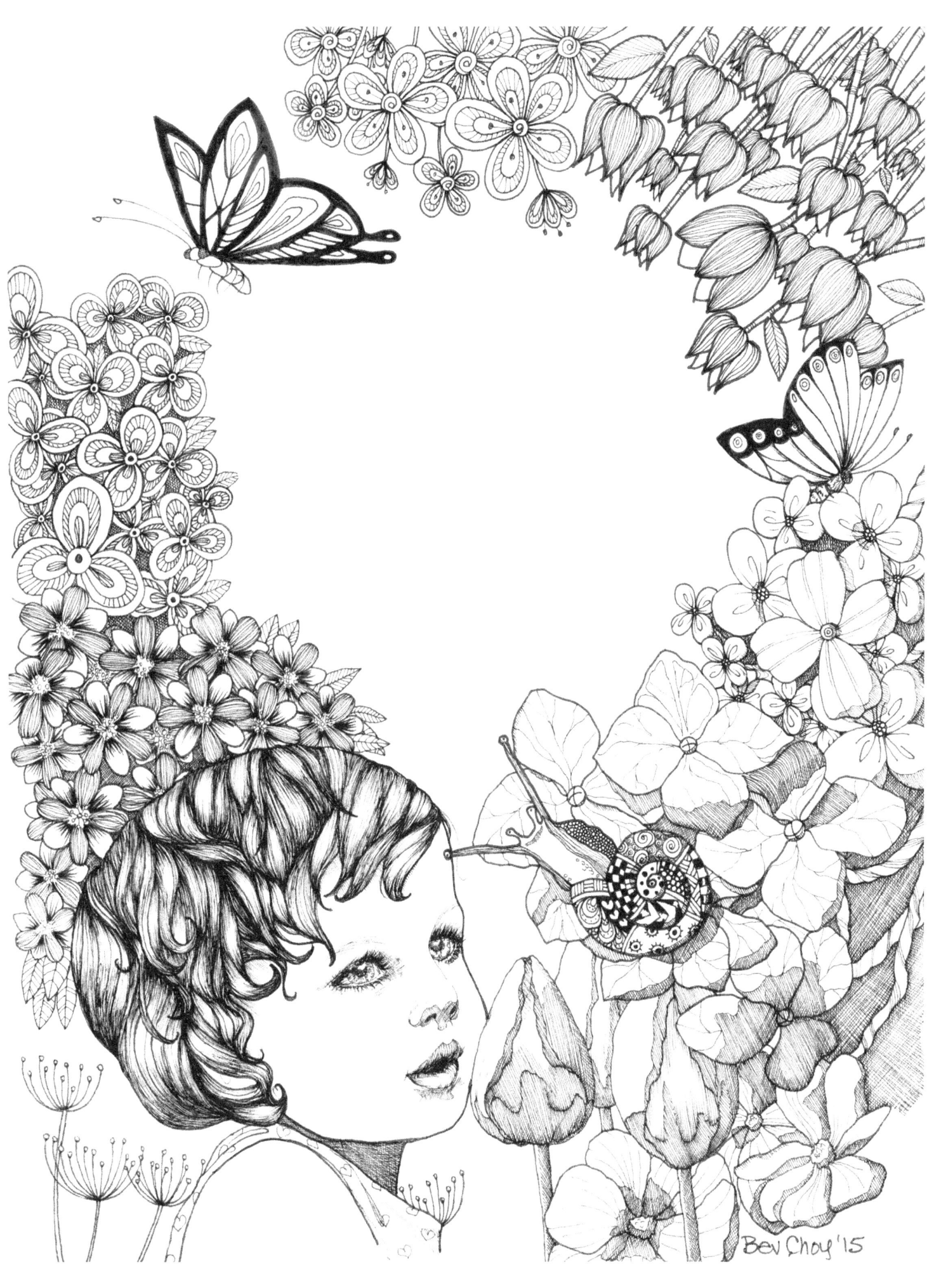

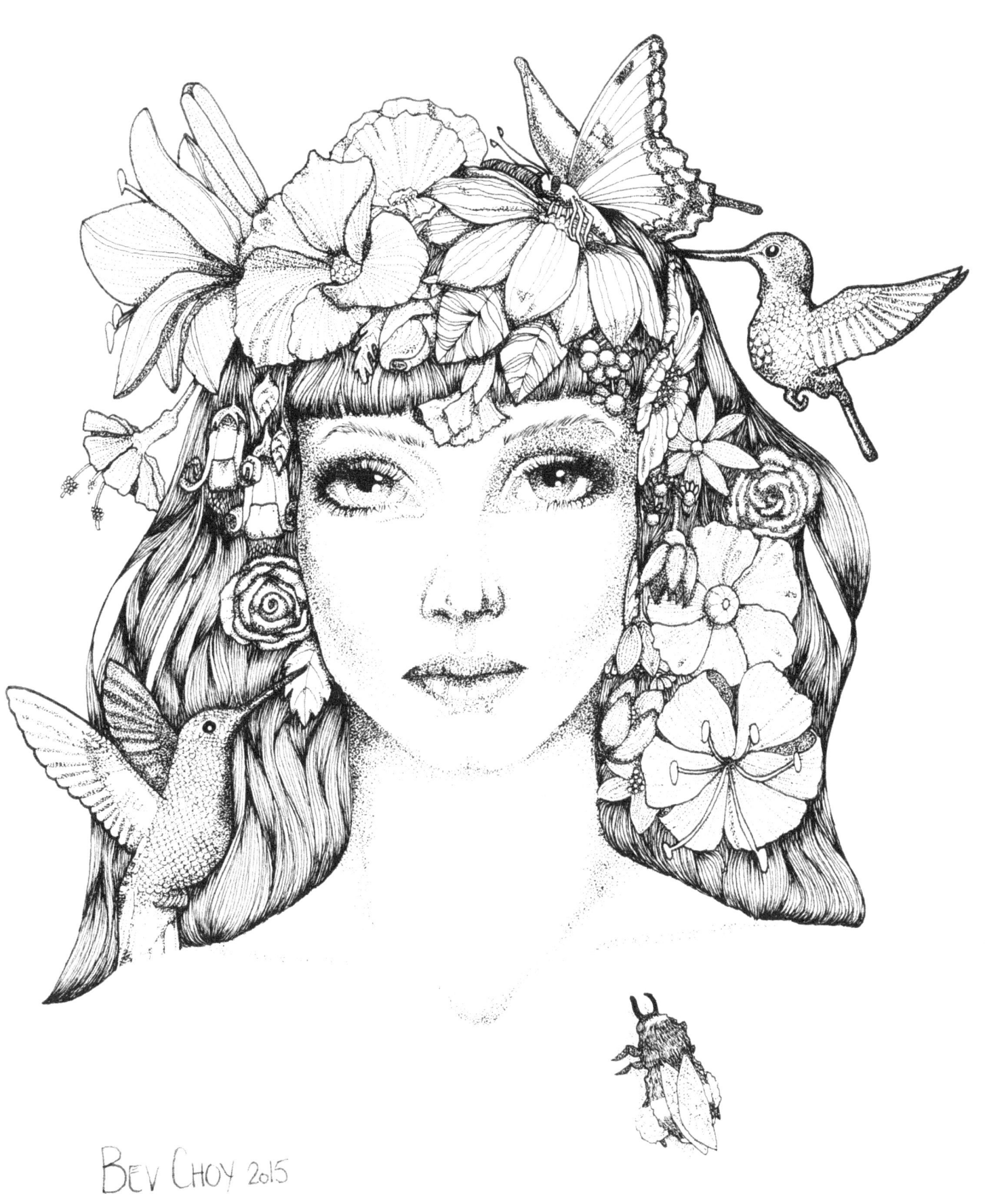

Bev Choy 2015

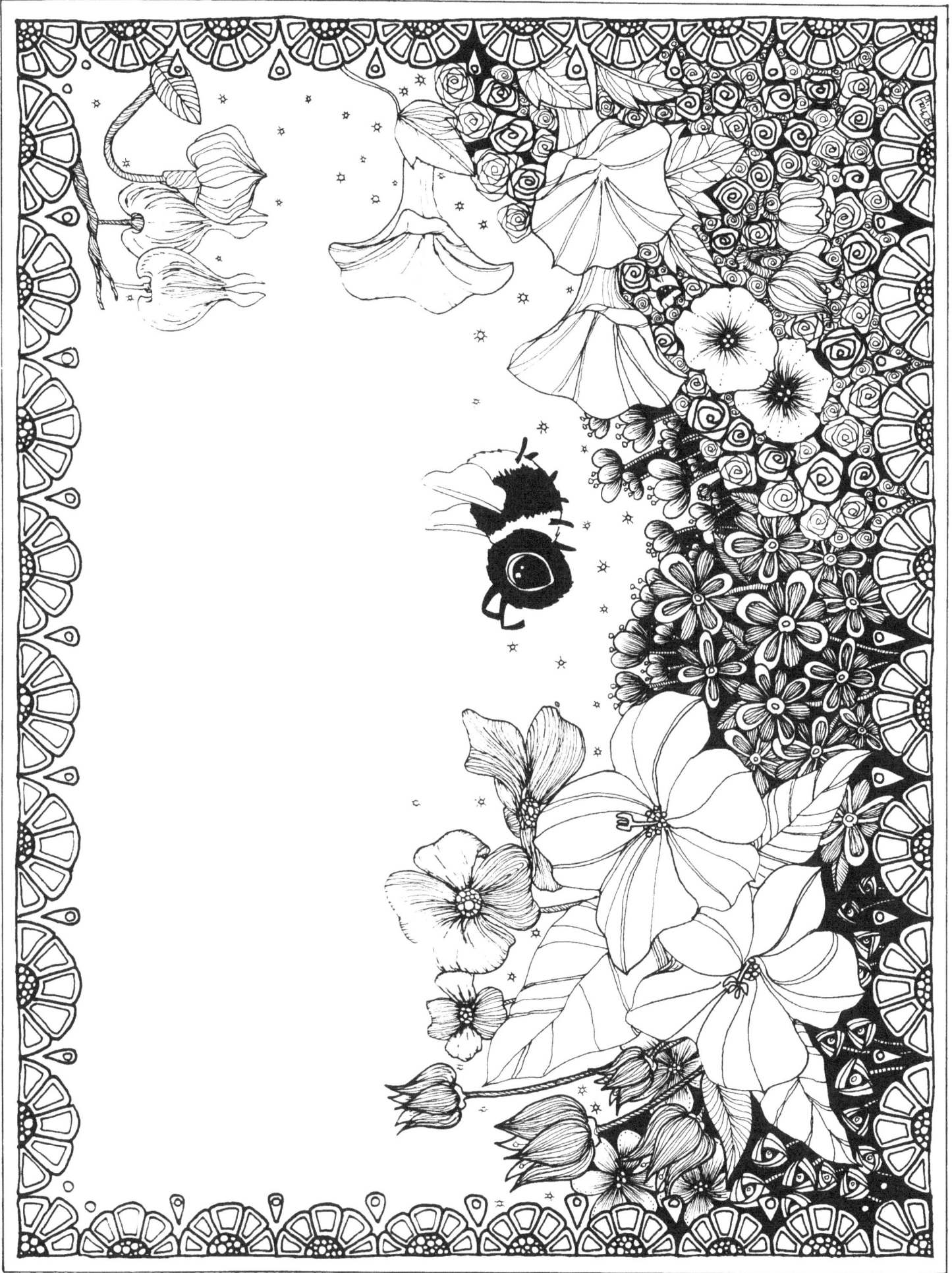

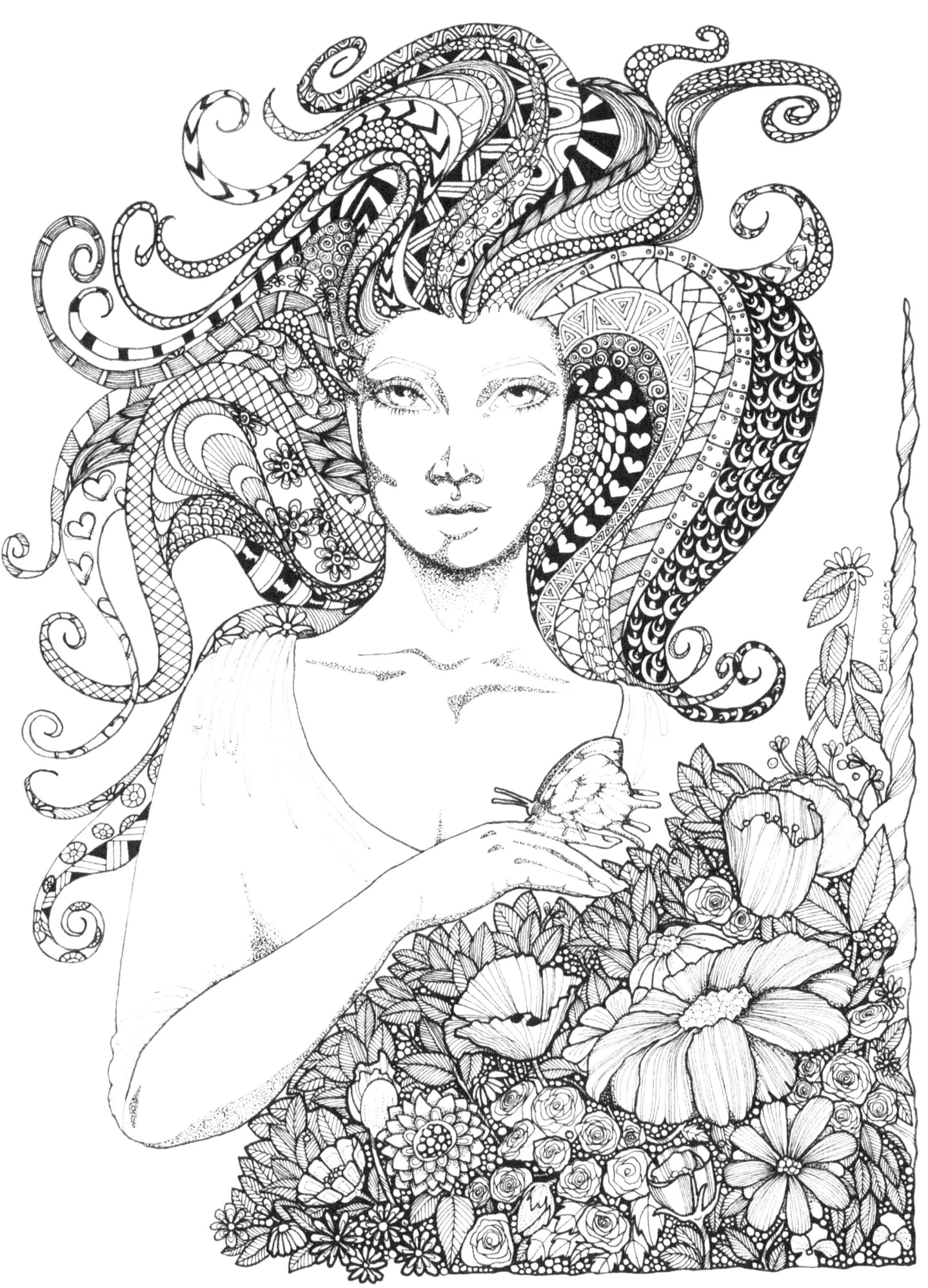

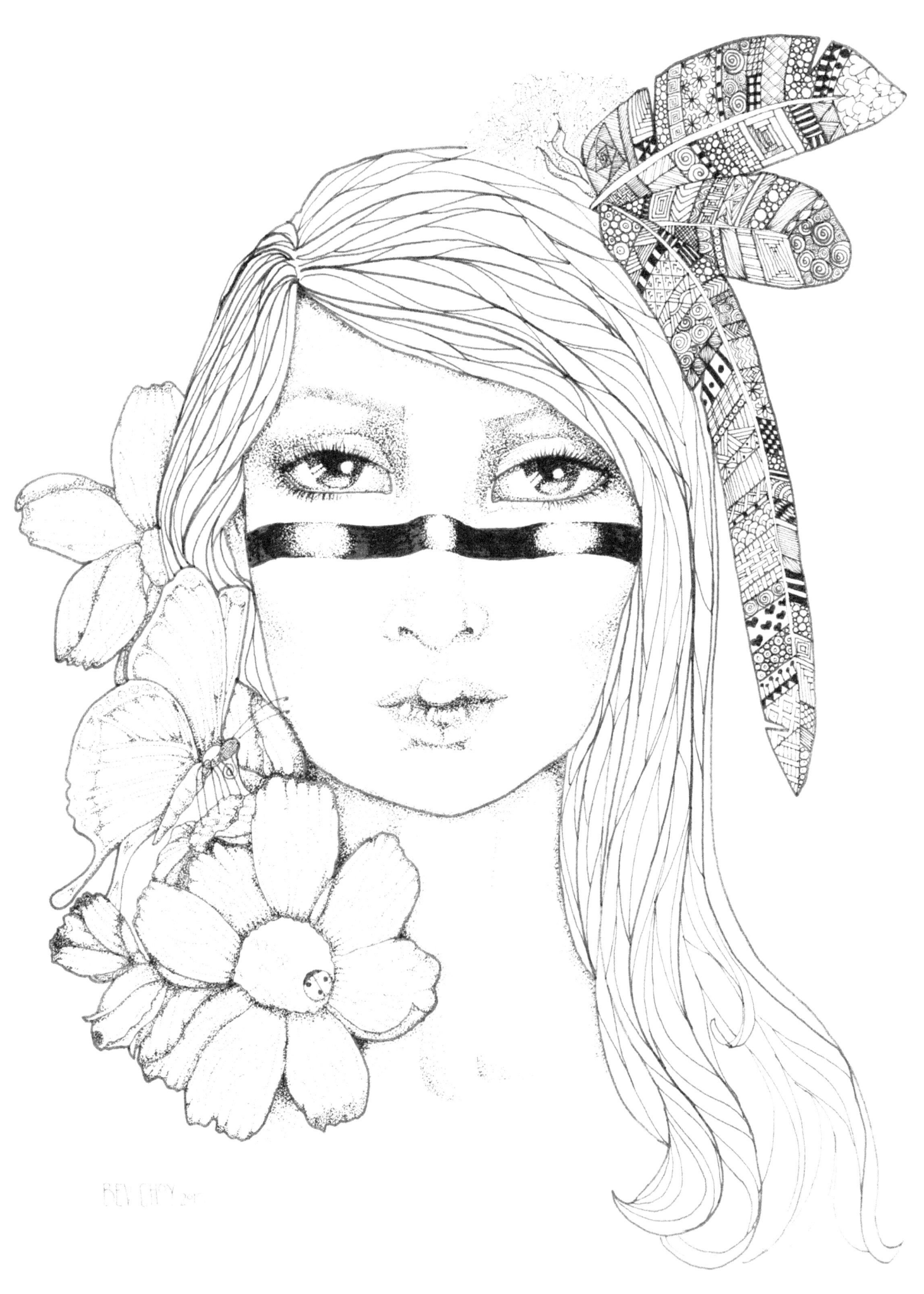

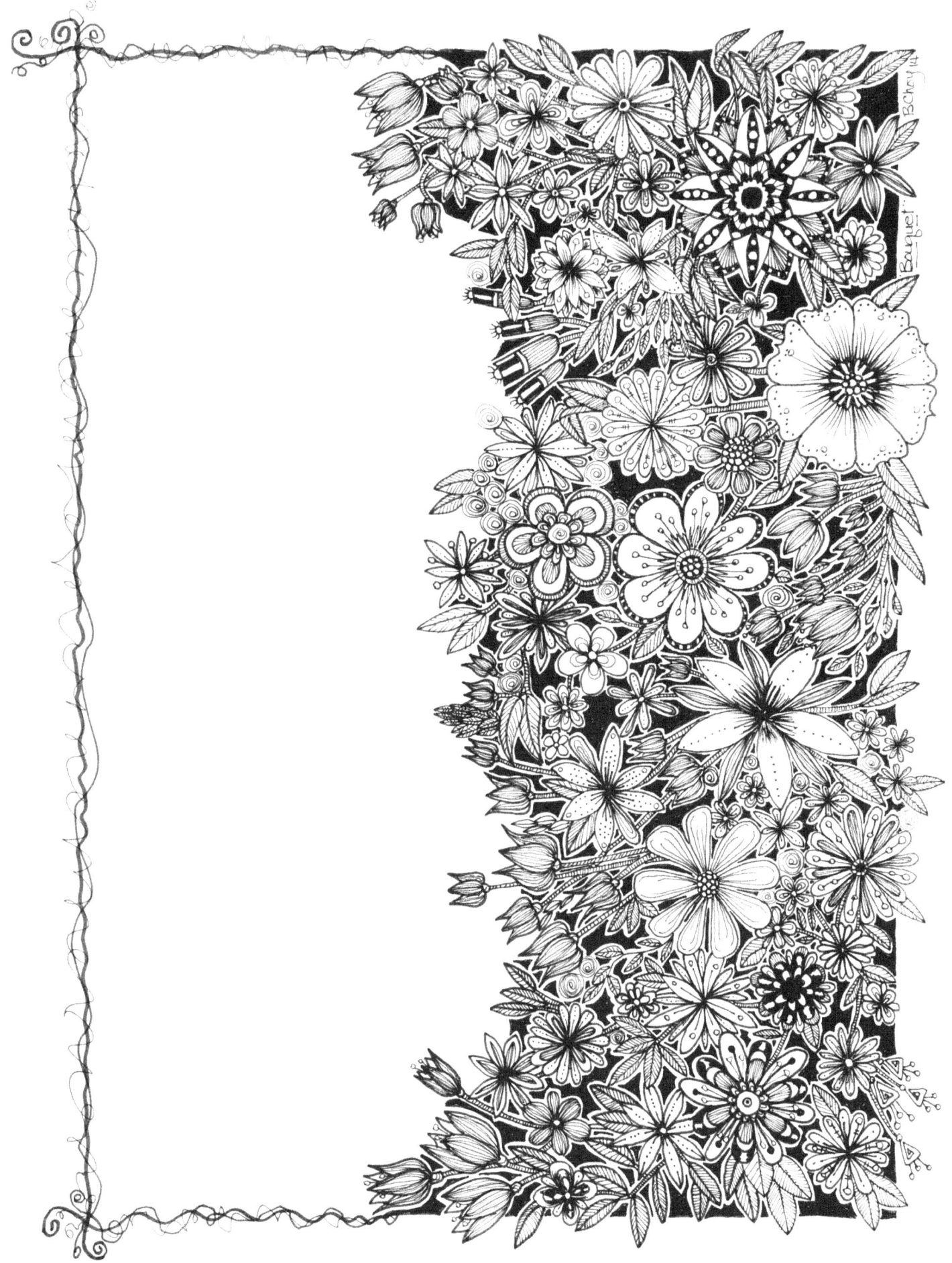

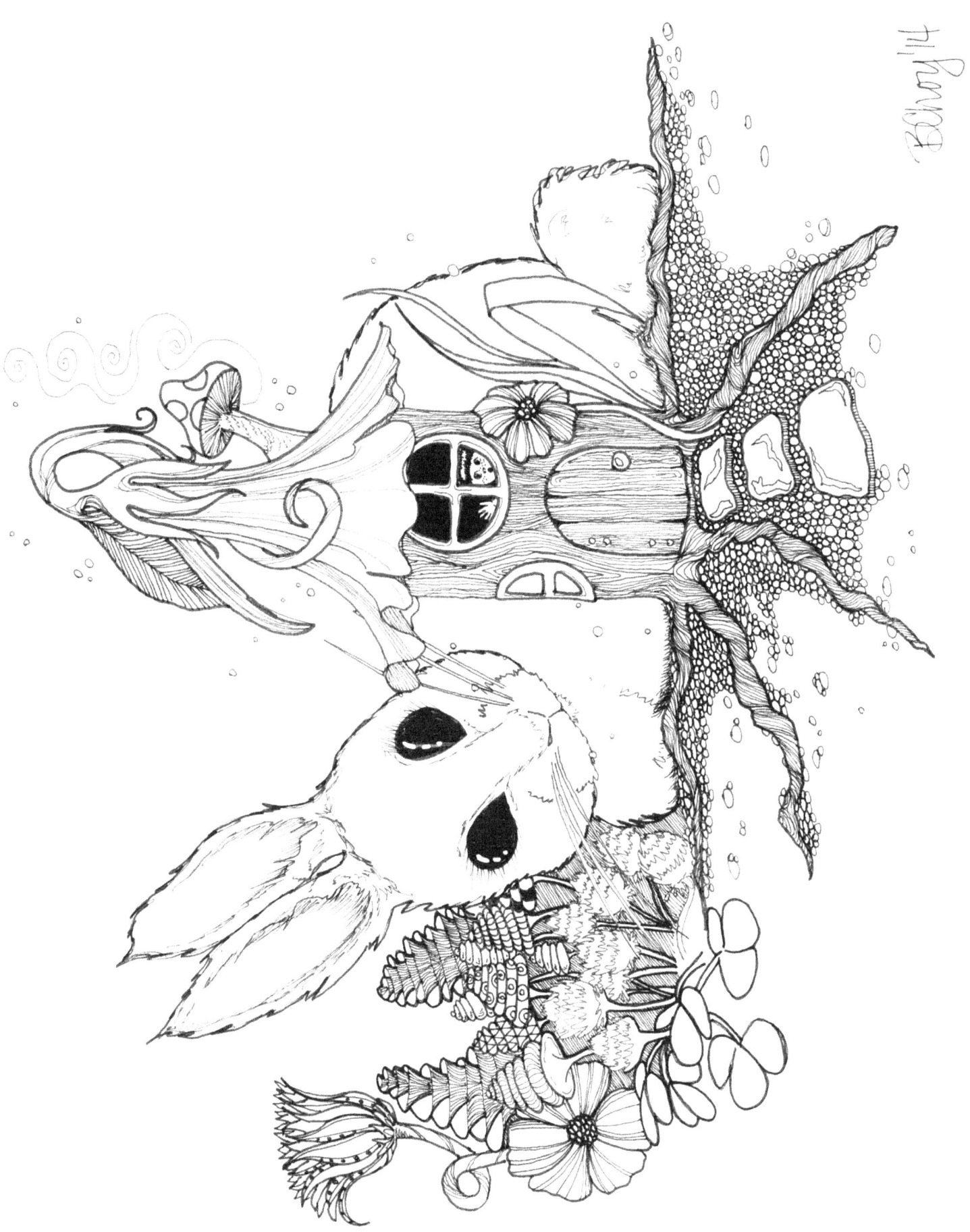

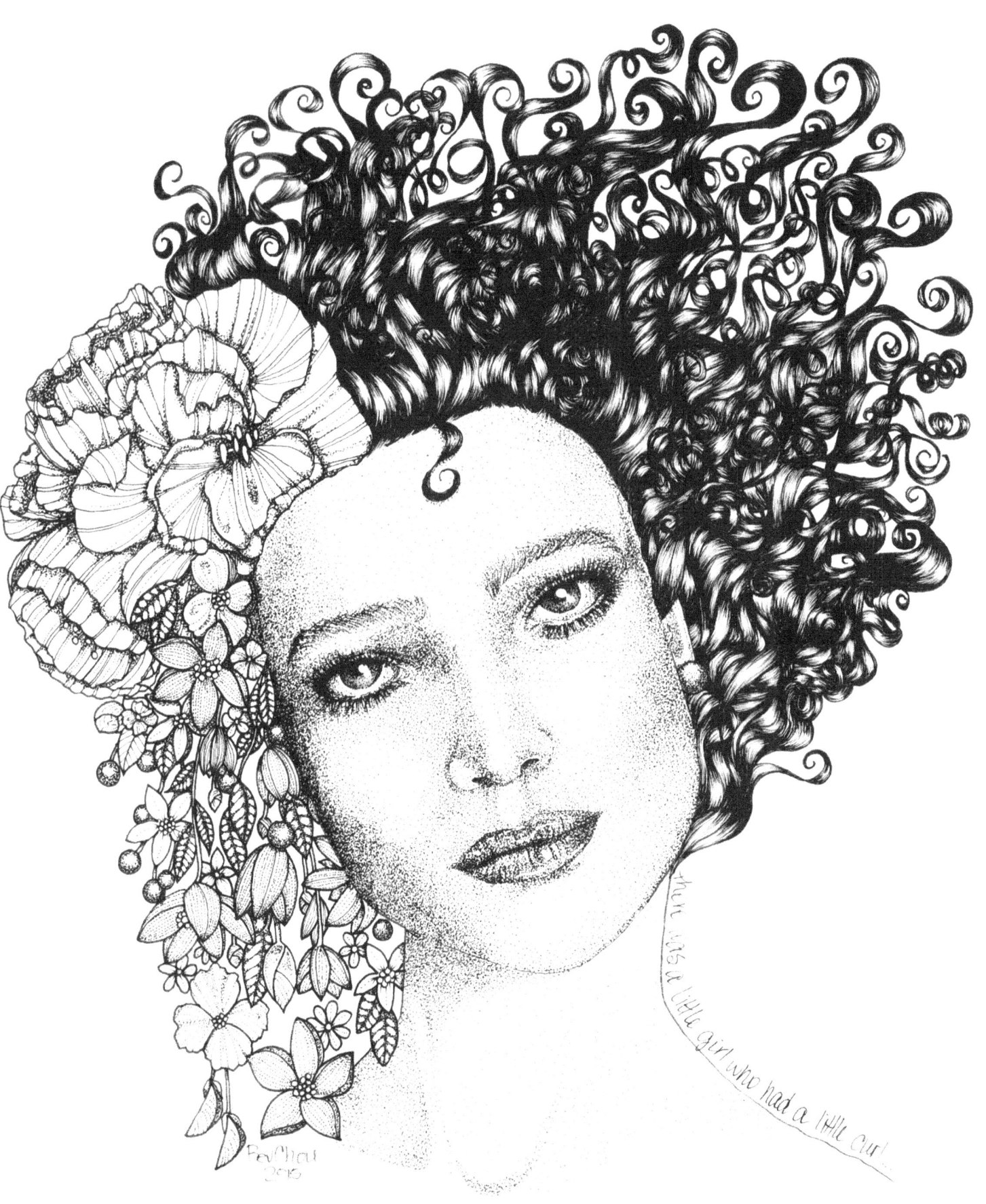

there was a little girl who had a little curl...

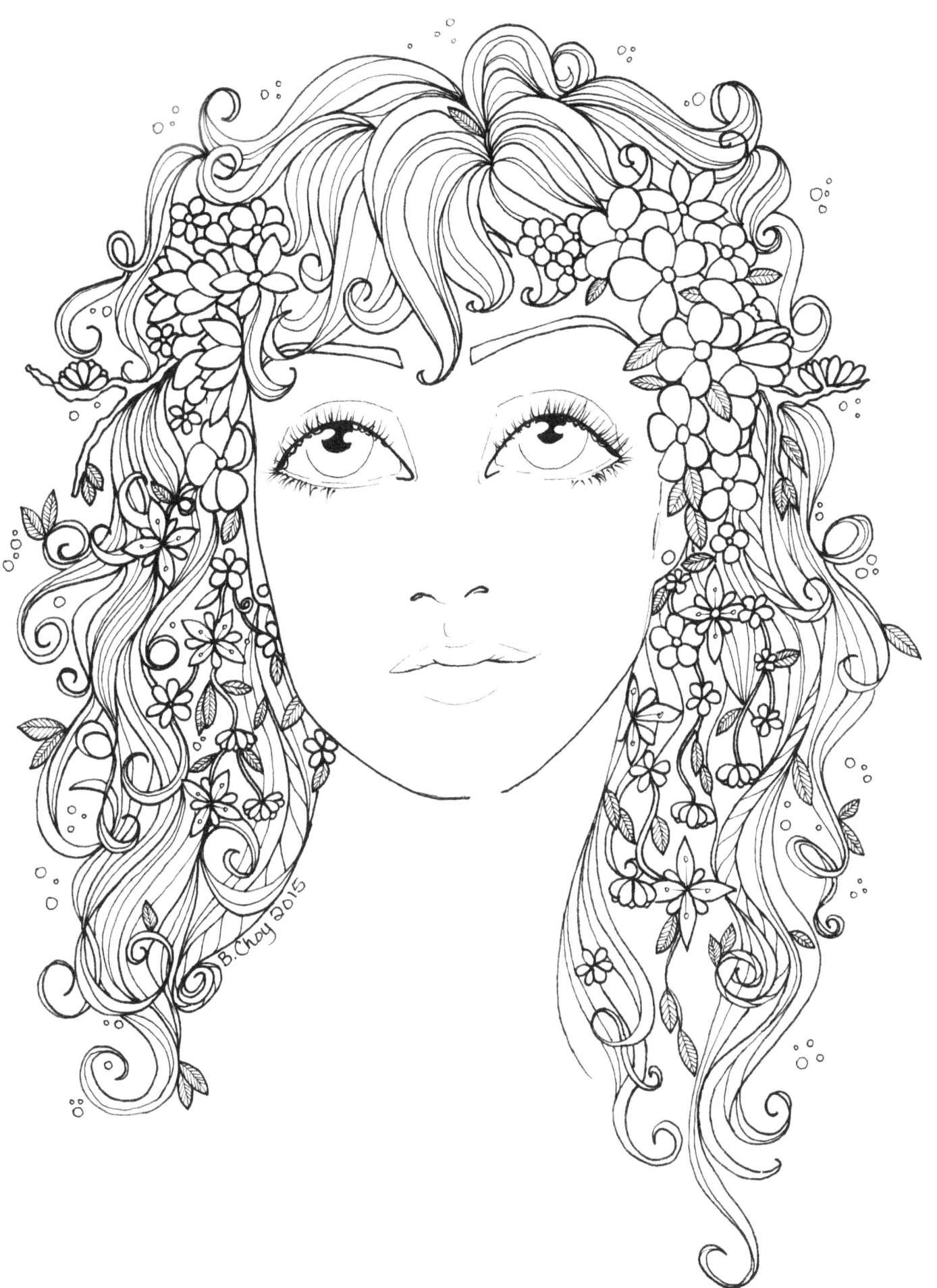

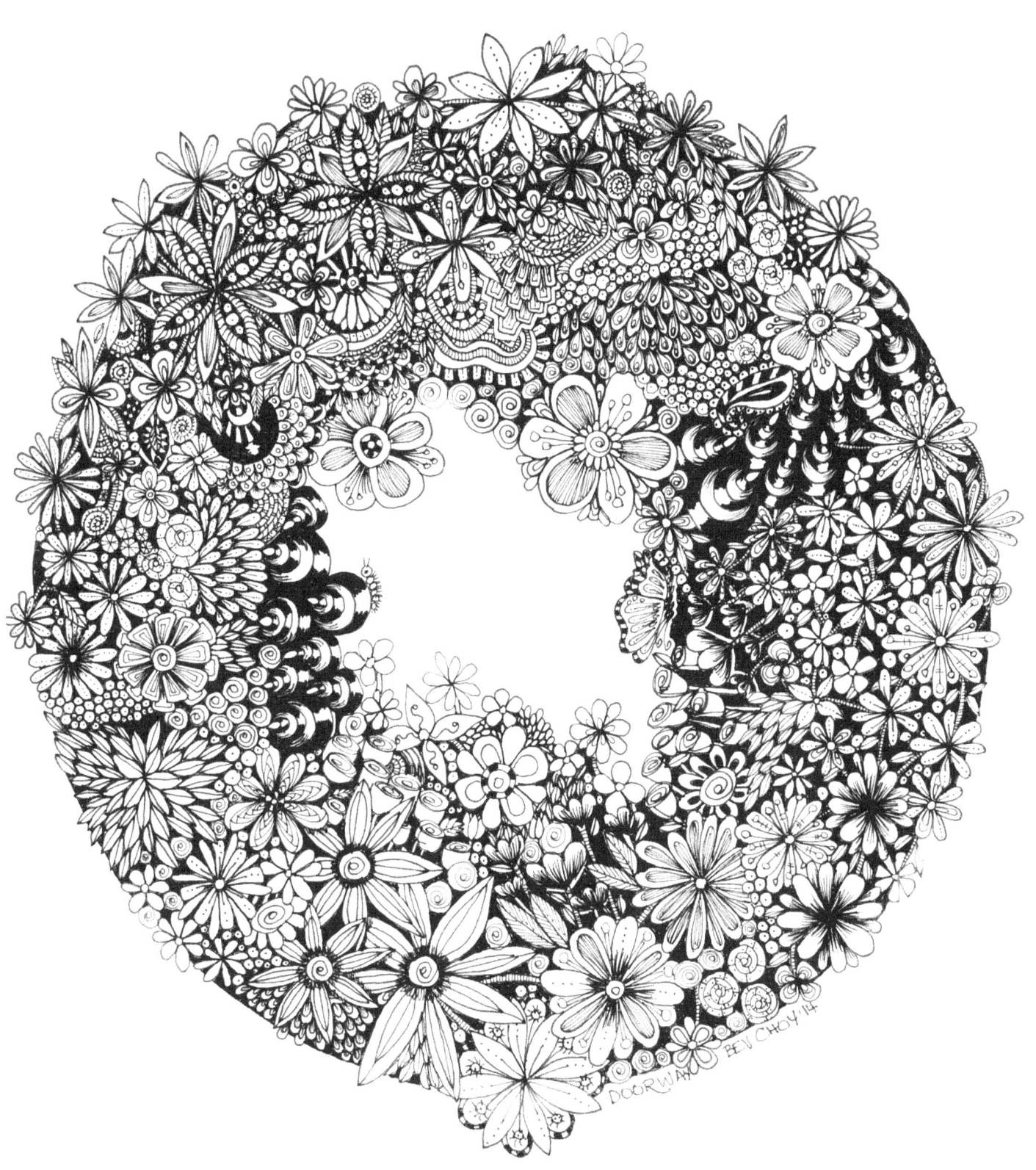

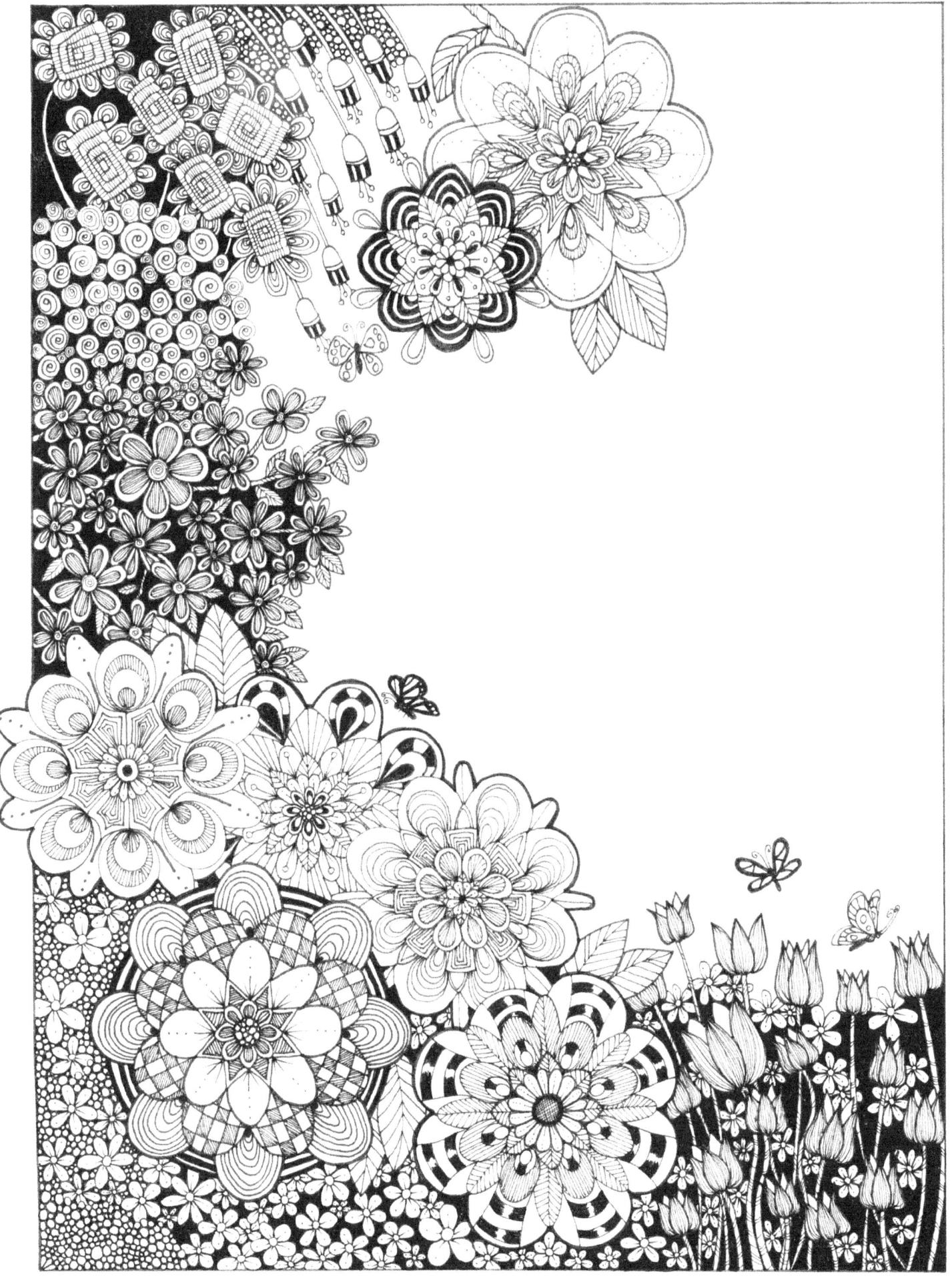

www.ingramcontent.com/pod-product-compliance
Lightning Source LLC
Chambersburg PA
CBHW080645180526
45168CB00008B/3315

* 9 7 8 1 5 1 4 7 9 9 2 8 4 *